MW00364229

Mozart's Grace

Mozart's Grace

SCOTT BURNHAM

Princeton University Press

Princeton and Oxford

press.princeton.edu

Library of Congress Cataloging-in-Publication Data

Burnham, Scott G.
Mozart's grace / Scott Burnham.
p. cm.
Includes bibliographical references and index.
ISBN 978-0-691-00910-0 (hardcover)
1. Mozart, Wolfgang Amadeus, 1756–1791—Criticism and interpretation.   I. Title.

ML410.M9B974 2013
780.92—dc23   2012030026

British Library Cataloging-in-Publication Data is available

This book has been composed in Sabon LT Std

Book designed by Marcella Engel Roberts

Printed on acid-free paper. ∞

Printed in the United States of America

1 3 5 7 9 10 8 6 4 2

For my favorite Mozart-loving angels, here and elsewhere:
Evalyn Foote Burnham
Luisa Heyl Foote

CONTENTS

Acknowledgments   ix

Invitation   1

I   Beauty and Grace   7

II   Thresholds   37

III   Grace and Renewal   117

Knowing Innocence   165

Notes   171
Bibliography   183
Index   187

ACKNOWLEDGMENTS

IN SOME SENSE THIS PROJECT BEGAN about thirty years ago, in the company of my old friend Jeff West, as we marveled together at various passages in Mozart's music. One that stood out in particular for us was the stunning return to the theme in the middle of the Adagio from the String Quintet in D Major, K. 593. Some fifteen years later, I revisited that passage in a paper called "Rehearing Mozart," delivered in honor of Edward T. Cone's eightieth birthday, in which I pondered how it is that we can rehear our favorite musics over and over again with enhanced enjoyment. Next, in November of 2001, I participated in "Music and the Aesthetics of Modernity," a conference in honor of Reinhold Brinkmann at Harvard University, where I presented "On the Beautiful in Mozart," a paper that became the prototype for this book.

On that occasion I was the grateful recipient of invaluable feedback and encouragement from Karol Berger and Anthony Newcomb, who organized the conference and edited the proceedings in a *Festschrift* for Reinhold (*Music and the Aesthetics of Modernity*, Harvard University Press, 2005), and also from Hans Ulrich Gumbrecht, Robert Levin, David Lewin, Lewis Lockwood, Charles Rosen, James Webster, and especially Reinhold Brinkmann himself, who upon publication of the essays, and in the midst of a debilitating illness, sent me a note of thanks with faltering handwriting but unwavering generosity and warmth of spirit.

Since then, I have been fortunate enough to read several additional papers related to this project for colleagues at a variety of institutions, including Case Western Reserve University, Cornell University, Florida State University, Indiana University, Ohio State University, Peabody Conservatory, Pennsylvania State University, Rider University, Stanford University, the State University of New York at Stony Brook, Swarthmore College, and the universities of Alabama, Iowa, Michigan, Oklahoma, and Oslo. On these many occasions I was the beneficiary of the expertise and enthusiasm of friends and colleagues too plentiful to enumerate here. But I would like to single out a few special individuals: Joseph Kerman, who shared with me an unpublished paper on K. 453; Leo Treitler, whose genial public response to my talk "Supernatural Mozart" remains a highlight of my academic career; and Charles Rosen, whose discussions and performances of Mozart (both recorded and impromptu) have taught me much over the years.

I also benefited enormously from presenting various parts of this project at Princeton University: to Eric Clarke, Jonathan Cross, and Laurence Dreyfus, visiting members of the Oxford-Princeton Music Analysis Study Group; to the amazing community of spirits in our Society of Fellows in the Liberal Arts, including my friends Mary Harper, Carol Rigolot, and Susan Stewart; to Kofi Agawu and Joseph Straus, friends and fellow members of the Princeton Theory Group; and to receptive and engaged groups of students and colleagues in the Music Department, as part of our Music Theory Group and our Work in Progress Series.

I am grateful to several anonymous readers for Princeton University Press, who challenged and encouraged me. Getting detailed reactions from gifted musicians and thinkers is always a stimulating experience, doubly so when the music in question is that of Mozart. Karol Berger and Mary Hunter also read the first full draft of my manuscript, and both revealed a fine sense of what I was trying to achieve, even amid the imperfections of my initial attempt to do so. I am also grateful for the example they have provided in their own inspiring work on Mozart's music. And if it were only possible, I would pick up the phone right now and tell Wendy Allanbrook how crucially important her magical book *Rhythmic Gesture in Mozart* (University of Chicago Press, 1983) has been to me and to everyone else in the field.

A number of people at Princeton University Press have made this book better and kept it on track. These include Fred Appel, whose infinite patience encompassed being able to hear for years that the book was "just around the corner"; Jodi Beder, musician and copy editor, who applied a generously exacting ear to the voice leading of my prose; Karen Carter, who oversaw the entire process of publication with humane ministrations; and Sarah David, who cheerfully assisted with a wide range of details surrounding production.

Seth Cluett, Laura Hedden, and Sanna Pederson each helped me mull over variants of the book's title. Somangshu Mukherji drew up the music examples seemingly as effortlessly as Mozart composed them. And the extraordinary Jim Clark offered me invaluable help and support at a ticklish stage of the project.

Sometimes I simply can't believe how lucky I am in my colleagues, my friends, and my family. At home I am continually blessed with the rejuvenating presence of Emmett, Sophia, and Georgia, musical spirits all. But it is Dawna Lemaire to whom I am most profoundly indebted: Dawna, who was playing Mozart's Rondo in A Minor around the time I was writing the bulk of this book; Dawna, who always listens carefully to my takes on various musical passages and never fails to add an elevating thought that is both musically and humanly insightful; and Dawna, whom I do not deserve, never thank enough, and hope someday to live up to.

Mozart's Grace would have been impossible to write without sabbatical leaves supported by the John Simon Guggenheim Memorial Foundation and the National Humanities Center. The music examples in *Mozart's Grace* were drawn up with the kind permission of the *Neue Mozart Ausgabe*, on which we relied for everything except occasional piano reductions of instrumental textures.

Mozart's Grace

INVITATION

Anticipatory Pronouncements . . .

"Whoever has discovered Mozart even to a small degree and then tries to speak about him falls quickly into what seems rapturous stammering."[1] So reports Karl Barth, German theologian, notable Mozart lover—and the producer of a number of his own rapt assessments of the composer's art. Indeed, the sound of Mozart urges many critics to make pronouncements that invoke musical perfection and more: no less a skeptic than Bernard Shaw said that Mozart's was "the only music yet written that would not sound out of place in the mouth of God."[2] Donald Francis Tovey strikes a more Christ-like note: "[Mozart] died young, and he touched no problem without solving it to perfection."[3] Mozart's proximity to divinity is claimed by these and others without hesitation or embarrassment—it is hard to imagine saying such things about any other composer, apart from Bach. Barth even felt it necessary to distinguish between the divine qualities of Bach and Mozart: "It may be that when the angels go about their task of praising God, they play only Bach. I am sure, however, that when they are together *en famille*, they play Mozart and that then too our dear Lord listens with special pleasure."[4] Bach, then, is always on the job, but when the agents of divinity go off duty, they turn to Mozart, as to the sounds of familial love and joy.

Others, without making direct reference to the divine, have heard Mozart's music as emanating from a heightened prospect. Schubert confided to his diary that Mozart offers "comforting perceptions of a brighter and better life"; Wagner spoke of Mozart as "music's genius of light and love."[5] Ferruccio Busoni, who authored several pages of aphorisms about Mozart on the occasion of his 150th birthday (1906), claimed "serene cheer" as the composer's "predominant feature."[6] Brighter, lighter, lovelier, happier—Mozart's music stands above the fray. As musicologist Alfred Einstein avers, in the final sentence of his biography of Mozart: "here is pure sound, conforming to a weightless cosmos, triumphant over all chaotic earthliness."[7]

The sonic purity Einstein values becomes Music Itself in the view of Karl Barth: "Could it be that the characteristic basic 'sound' of both the earlier and later Mozart—not to be confused with the sound of any other—is in fact the primal sound of music absolutely? Could it be that he discovered and struck this 'tone' in its timelessly valid form?"[8] Here we have moved all the way up to a Platonic Mozart, the ideal from which all other musics fall off into contingent realities. Paul Henry Lang translates this sense of unrivalled superiority into the language of aesthetic objectivity:

> Mozart is the greatest musico-dramatic genius of all times. This unique position he owes to a temperament which approached everything, every situation, and every human being with absolute objectivity. . . . Every situation and every individual appeared to him as music, his whole conception was purely aesthetic, and music was his language. He preserved the old and great virtues of Italian music, and in his universal genius these united with German transcendentalism, embodying the plans, desires, and hopes of the outgoing century.[9]

What doesn't Mozart achieve in Lang's exalted summation? Here we encounter the universal, objective Mozart, an aesthetic god in his dispassionate handling of all things human, forging the link from Western music's past to its future. Barth too posits a godlike Mozart who keeps life and death, heaven and earth "ever present before his eyes, in his hearing, and in his heart." Barth continues: "Knowing all, Mozart creates music from a mysterious center, and so knows and observes limits to the right and the left, above and below. He maintains moderation."[10] Barth's great themes concerning Mozart's music are Play and Freedom; it is as though the composer can place himself at the calm center of the human universe, freely and playfully translating into music the multifarious parade of humanity spinning around him.[11]

Wherever one positions Mozart in the cosmography of human perfectibility, one thing remains unquestioned: we place absolute trust in Mozart's musical judgment, as in no other's. He seems a kind of aesthetic tuning fork, incapable of a poorly voiced sonority, a misjudged line, an overworked effect. And not only do we trust him, but who among us has not experienced wonder at his unerring mastery? Other things in which we invest both trust and wonder include what we can observe of the great rhythms of nature: the phases of the moon, the orbits of the moons of Jupiter, the appointed rounds of celestial objects. But these are distant worlds, far removed from the circle of human intimacy, while Mozart's music is somehow both unerring and human. Why is this combination not disturbingly uncanny, or supremely off-putting? In my own case, it has partly to do with an emotional reaction that often ambushes me when I pay closer attention to Mozart's music. This is the same reflex that can bring tears to the eyes when listening to Bach, or Art Tatum: in the presence of such joyful abundance and facility, such superhuman play, I am not floored with overawed admiration, but rather find myself glad to be alive, overjoyed to be in the same world with such sounds.

Trust, Wonder, Joy. No surprise that Mozart's music is often treated as an unfailingly good thing, a beneficial presence—like light, or warmth. Unlike the sublime infallibility of great celestial bodies, light and warmth can be brought into one's own circle and—in moderation—can always and only be good. For Mozart's much vaunted evenhandedness ensures that the light will never glare nor the warmth sear. Yet the effect of Mozart's music goes beyond the comforts of a well-moderated environment. Rather, one welcomes Mozart's music as one welcomes certain gratifying effects of light and warmth, such as the smell of fresh baked bread, or the surging smile of a loved one.

But metaphors of creature comfort, and even of human love, will never quite capture the special experience many of us have when listening to Mozart. For this we may need to draw closer to a sense of enchantment, by invoking that quality of Mozart's music that everyone asserts but almost no one discusses: unsurpassed beauty. That Mozart composed the most beautiful music we can know is an article of faith among listeners and critics of Mozart's music. And like other articles of faith, it is rarely if ever held up to scrutiny. Most musically trained critics are content simply to acknowledge the sheer beauty of this music as they move off to more tractable topics. A recent exception that proves the general rule can be found in Maynard Solomon's 1995 biography of Mozart, in which he devotes two entire chapters to a probing interpretation of the beautiful in Mozart's music. But for most others, those in the rank and file of academia as well as millions of music-loving civilians, the beauty of Mozart's music is simply taken for granted, as a happy boon, one of the few things in life that do not need to be questioned or examined but only enjoyed. Or commodified—in the form of the so-called "Mozart Effect," a kind of spiritual balm that enhances the growth of house plants, increases the intelligence of children about to take tests, and generally leads the troubled modern mind to a semblance of serenity.[12]

. . . Toward an Enchanted Appreciation

In what follows, I too wish to speak of the Mozart effect, but unlike more commercial proponents I do not wish to leave it unexamined. Instead, I have composed what might best be called an appreciation, a personal attempt to describe what is striking about the sound of Mozart. In making this attempt, I deploy simple analytical accounts of musical effects, but always also relate these effects to other domains of human significance. The musico-aesthetic issues I will address include sonority, texture, line, harmony, dissonance, and timing, as well as aspects of large-scale form such as thematic returns, retransitions, and endings. In conjunction with these many musical instances I will explore qualities of expression, intimation, interiority, innocence, melancholy, grace, and renewal.

Above all, I wish to apprehend the quality of beauty in Mozart's music. Until recently, such an agenda would likely have appeared naïve and obsolete. Scholars and critics engaged with the arts had long outgrown the notion of beauty, dismissing it as a moldering aesthetic category, an uncritical pledge to some fantasy of "immanence"—or, worse yet, as a trivializing assessment signifying little more than "pretty." Nowadays, theories of beauty are once again flourishing in various quarters.[13] And while I myself am neither equipped nor inclined to make a philosophical argument for the importance of acknowledging beauty, I would like to think that my treatment of Mozart's music could function in support of such an argument, or at least that any such argument would do well to consider the remarkable bearing of Mozartean beauty.

For the beautiful in Mozart seems to stand apart, untouched by human hands. Which is to say that Mozart's music often seems effortless, an aesthetic judgment often ratified by what we know of the circumstances of its composition. Human strain, or even overt human manipulation, the tooling of a product, would seem to have left little mark here. The music seems somehow pre-made, and it glows with a self-sufficiency that has less to do with "unity" and more with apartness: untouched, untouchable. It is often heard as a kind of alabaster that flows without perturbation—this effect has nothing to do with a lack of dramatic events in the music but rather with the bearing of the music, for even the most electrifyingly dissonant passages never cloy; the psychic envelope of the music never threatens to tear; nothing is going to burst. Yet even so, the effect is not that of some distant Olympian but is often as moving as Schubert. What musical features account for this particular kind of beauty? Why do we tend to hear Mozart's music as both untouchable and touching? Questions like these will inflect my discussion of sonority and line in the opening chapter of the book, in which we will first encounter beauty as though held in suspension, and then beauty as though placed in motion, becoming grace.

In the central chapter, I will make much of the Romantic idea of liminal states, arguing that Mozart often stages the uncanny threshold of another dimension, whether deeply interior or incipiently transcendent, by composing passages that seem to rise above the discourse of their surroundings. Many of these will involve oblique, out-of-phase dissonance, or so-called "purple patches" arising from the middle of a phrase. Such passages will also be heard to signal a move away from Enlightenment certainties toward the less certain but more enticing attractions of Modernity. And in the third chapter, I will try to account for an intuitive sense of grace and renewal that infuses Mozart's music at moments of formal consequence, such as his way of seeming to arrest the flow of time during retransitions. As the book draws to a close, my observations will be increasingly tinged with references to ironic self-consciousness, as an analogy to the reflexive buoyancy of Mozart's music. In the epilogue I will try to gather some of these themes under the sign of "knowing innocence," an ingratiating and renewable modality of spirit fostered through the Mozart experience.

While my approach may seem to entail an ambitious reach, much about Mozart's music will remain outside the penumbra of this short book: there will be nothing on his compositional process and no attempt toward comprehensive coverage of his every genre or formal type. And though I hope that performers of Mozart's music will be in the front ranks of my audience, I will not presume to suggest ways to realize his music, nor will I analyze any existing performances. Given these disclosures, one might suspect that my project is rather more self-indulgent than systematic, nor would it be incorrect to do so: my initial motivation was in fact the urge to write about many of my favorite passages. In the face of one of his own cherished spots in Mozart, Tovey once said this: "Mozart . . . has uttered one of those sublimities which are incomparable with each other and with everything else, except as touchstones for one's own sense of beauty."[14] I like to think of the passages I have selected here as my own set of Mozartean touchstones. My aim in considering these touchstones has been a simple one: listen closely and describe their effects as I hear them. I do this in part to support some of the reigning critical intuitions about Mozart's music with fresh analytical evidence, and in part to develop a newly inflected view of our perennial susceptibility to his music.

Though such an analysis may serve to demystify some aspects of Mozart's music, I have no interest in disenchanting the experience. Quite the opposite: I would rather enter into a kind of knowing enchantment. Scholars working hard on the broad and complex front lines of musicological inquiry may well regard my enterprise as a retreat into some hopelessly Romantic engagement with the musical experience, as though to escape reality by drifting into an enchanted realm. Yet I believe we all inhabit such realms, whether we acknowledge it or not: even the most resolutely disenchanted among us maintain any number of welcome illusions in order to sustain such a resolution. So I invite you to share my enchanted appreciation of Mozart, my ongoing embrace of the illusions of beauty and grace.[15] If you feel you can accept this invitation, may our time together be well spent.

BEAUTY AND GRACE

Anmut ist eine bewegliche Schönheit . . .
[Grace is Beauty astir . . .]

Schiller, Über Anmut und Würde

Die Schönheit bleibt sich selber selig;
Die Anmut macht unwiderstehlich . . .
[Beauty's delighted with itself;
Grace makes it irresistible . . .]

Goethe, Faust Part II, lines 7403–4[1]

Sonority

What is so special about the sound of Mozart? Consider the opening of the Adagio from the Clarinet Concerto, much beloved for its pellucid beauty (example 1.1). There is nothing the least bit exotic in the first four-bar phrase. Everything is transparent, straightforward: simple harmonies (tonic and dominant), guileless melody, slow harmonic rhythm. And yet there is a force at work that holds this texture together in beautiful suspension, a focal energy that creates a sense of apartness and integrity. Note first the warmly cohesive, floating quality of the string sonority: the pedal tone in the viola sustains the sound, while the murmuring figures in the violins lend it a gentle animation—the contrary motion of their figuration promotes a sense of balanced individuation. Then consider the bass line, which works in tandem with the harmonic rhythm: its brief nudges on the dominant give the texture just enough push to keep it floating, but not so much as to force anything. That the dominant falls on

Example 1.1. Clarinet Concerto, K. 622, ii, bars 1–32

Example 1.1 (*Cont.*)

the downbeat and not on the preceding upbeat subtly undermines the downbeat as an arrival and contributes to the effect of a floating, suspended tonic.

Above this texture, the clarinet melody opens a calm triadic space, reaching from the fifth A through the root D to the third F-sharp. As the radiant "color tone" of the triad, this F-sharp emerges as a small extravagance. Its flight is brief: touched by the fleeting dominant harmony with the barest hint of dissonance, the F-sharp is drawn back down to the root D. Its life-span is as the top of an arc, a passing zenith. The utterance that follows takes a further step upward by riding the triadic arc to its next valence, the fifth, A, which also then recedes over a dominant harmony, settling on the F-sharp. The energy for this incremental expansion is gained by holding the initial, lower-register A for an additional eighth note, a subtle instance of *reculer pour mieux sauter*. But "leaping" seems too strong, too directed, for the quality of this motion: this is more a graceful play of swelling arcs, the triad stretching pleasantly in its warm surroundings.

In the next four-bar phrase (bars 5–8), the harmonic center of gravity shifts from tonic to dominant, while the clarinet melody first dallies with E and then plunges into a sinuous gesture more varied in shape and intervallic content than anything before. This brief intervallic intensification works in conjunction with the overall harmonic trajectory of the passage, contributing to a gentle surge of energy that brings about a cadence on the dominant. Repeating the entire eight-bar phrase with the addition of wind instruments and with violins on the melody (bars 9–16) infuses it with fresh sonority, amplifying this intimate utterance in the same way that a strong breeze transforms the stillness of a forest.

The energy of this opening passage is largely focused on maintaining its sonorous envelope, on enforcing a special centeredness that—like a spinning top—seems to create its own field of gravity, apart from the pull of functional syntax. In this and other such passages in Mozart, the rhythmic relation between pulsing accompaniment and slower moving melody creates an animated stillness.[2] (To get a precise sense of how the oscillating string figures contribute to this effect, try substituting either an Alberti bass pattern or simple repeated chords underneath the melody.) The entire passage hums with the exquisite tension of keeping things in suspension. This suspension of mundane musical reality—and by means of the most transparent elements of that reality—fosters a special awareness in the listener, creating an expectant yet relaxed state of mind.

And then, as if gathering and channeling the atmospheric energy of this opening, the music moves into a gently charged sequence, with three rising stations and a diversified cast of supporting harmonies (bars 17–24). Each two-bar station is heard as an intensification, as the clarinet launches stepwise descents from F-sharp, then from G, and finally from

A. Thus the A touched so easily in the first eight-bar phrase is now the top stair of a more deliberate procession. Stepping back down from this A, the clarinet enters into an elaborate four-bar descent that both recovers the space opened in the slow ascending sequence and answers the move to the dominant at the end of the first long phrase. This eight-bar line completes the broadest arc yet; and like the earlier phrase, it too is ratified by a fuller orchestra.

The entire opening tableau of the Adagio records a transformation from a sense of suspension to one of intensification. The bated breath of the first sixteen bars is answered by the deeply drawn breaths of the sequence and its aftermath. An overall tonal balance has been achieved, for the concluding tonic cadences in bars 24 and 32 settle the medial cadences on the dominant in bars 8 and 16. Meanwhile, the ascending melodic impulse that starts in bar 17 elaborates the cumulative ascent from F-sharp to A in the opening phrases of the first section, now with a sequence that climbs stepwise through the same interval—and both these ascents are answered by concluding descents back to D. A series of ingratiating arcs, undulations at different levels, shapes the melodic flow, while the repetition of each phrase creates another kind of undulation, one that obtains between the intimacy of the solo clarinet and the animating support of the orchestra.

Similar qualities suffuse what may well be the single most beautiful number in all of Mozart's operas, the farewell trio "Soave sia il vento" from *Così fan tutte* (example 1.2). Here three Mozartean characters—two "innocent" women and an older, self-professed "man of the world"—find themselves suspended within some suprapersonal emotional dimension, well beyond the puppet-stage confines of their comic misery (the feigned departure of the women's boyfriends, a ruse devised by the older man in order to test their fidelity). That Mozart's music takes no notice of the comic feigning and instead registers at the level of a sincere farewell allows its beauty to be rarer still, as when some mundane action suddenly triggers a vastly moving sense of what it means to be human. On the mundane level of this scene, two of the singing characters think they are taking leave of their boyfriends, while we in the audience (along with the worldly manipulator onstage) know better. But Mozart's music seems to know something else entirely: though the depicted leave taking is not genuine, there is a farewell sounding here that exceeds the emotional depth even of a genuine parting of lovers—the characters seem to be taking leave of Innocence itself.

Like the Adagio from the Clarinet Concerto, "Soave sia il vento" creates its effect of beautiful suspension through simple harmonies, a slow harmonic rhythm, and murmuring string figures; moreover, it manages to maintain this special quality for the entire duration of a self-contained number.

Example 1.2 *Così fan tutte*, "Soave sia il vento"

Example 1.2 (*Cont.*)

Example 1.2 (*Cont.*)

Example 1.2 (Cont.)

Example 1.2 (Cont.)

Example 1.2 (Cont.)

Example 1.2 (*Cont.*)

The prevailing texture is much like the Adagio: again the violas sustain while muted violins gently animate slow exchanges of tonic and dominant; cellos and basses mark a slow beat on the roots of those harmonies. The sound of this opening seems to enchant the three singers, who begin as if transfixed.[3] Their voices form a "soave" envelope around the repeated string figures, with a sustained utterance that stretches to the downbeat of bar 4 before pausing. The timeless, otherworldly effect of this trio is due not only to the hushed sonic ambience but also to the different time scales enacted by violins, lower strings, and voices. Underneath the burbling sixteenth notes, pizzicati in the lower strings take on a relaxed temporal mien, marking every half bar. The harmonic rhythm of the opening moves at the even more relaxed pace of one chord per bar. And then the voices ask us to listen to a gesture that lasts for two bars. Thus the trio deepens into its slowness, its otherworldly pace and bearing.

Even the unassuming wave figures of the violins in the first two bars of this evocation of calm seas are progressively embedded temporally, as wavelets within waves. Immediate repetition marks the eighth-note level, pattern change marks the quarter-note level, larger-scale repetition marks the half-note level, and then descending sequence marks the whole-note level. Over and around this stylized wave environment the three voices form another kind of wave, lasting two bars and with an internally fluid shape, as the baritone crests first, followed by the soprano. Another two-bar vocal wave closes the first long tableau of tonic and dominant at bar 6. And again like the Adagio from the Clarinet Concerto, the opening section then gives way to an intensified passage featuring winds, the subdominant harmony, and a newly swelling melodic line.

Here the voices and wind instruments continue building waves, now smoother and more directed. These waves crest first in repeated two-bar arcs, topped by soprano F-sharps, then subside with a two-bar phrase that drops to a half cadence (bars 7–12). But this marked subsidence leads, as at the seashore, to the largest wave yet, four bars (bars 13–16) with an ascending upper voice that crests on a fleeting G-sharp, the zenith ninth of a sonority that tonicizes the dominant in a harmonic surge. Thus the biggest wave marks the most momentous arrival yet. Very different music follows: the strings stop their figurations, and a descending sequence with invertible counterpoint emerges, featuring a bewitching chromatic slide from A-sharp to A-natural. The invertible counterpoint allows the baritone line to descend over the full range of the passage, while the women trade off singing the top-voice arcs. This exchange colors the sequence with two different voice types on these wavelike figures that reach up to F-sharp, then up to E, as though letting us down gradually from the big wave's G-sharp crest. The next two bars make as though to settle cadentially back onto E.

At the point where this motion would normatively find that cadence on E (bar 22), something wonderful transpires, a magical passage that suspends the action and thus encapsulates the enchanted beauty of the entire trio, with a sound both otherworldly and sensuous.[4] The strings return to the whispering sixteenth notes, while a chromatic sonority (an A-sharp diminished seventh chord over the pedal B, followed by the home dominant seventh on B) interrupts the resolution with a fresh suffusion of sustained sound. If this weren't enough, the cadence sets up again and is again interrupted by the magical chord (bar 25), with soprano and baritone now switching parts, so that the soprano can start an ascent from the C-sharp that will go all the way up to G-sharp, while the baritone takes the A-sharp–A-natural route that will allow him to descend to E. Thus the repeated magic chord and its deft revoicing enable the climactic crest of the entire trio. The women's sustained G-sharp and E has a clarifying force: *this* top swell stays in place. Under the radiance of this sound, the baritone becomes a rhapsode, with a sinuous line that vaults up and drifts down—to which the women answer with a cadenza-like downward rush of thirds. After the baritone completes this cadenza with his own sixteenth-note run, a codetta begins, valediction to this valedictory trio. Here the women wave good-bye with gentle leaps (scale degrees 3–6–2–4–3) over a most benign cadential progression (by thirds: I–vi–ii⁶–V–I), three times repeated. And even now the leave-taking is not complete; the wind instruments wave twice again, as though wafting the departing ship's horn across the widening distance.

The trio stays in character throughout: the enchantment never wavers, but only deepens. The events we experience can be processed as distinct formal functions: gradual tipping to the dominant, pedal point, return with high point, cadenza, codetta. And yet the sonic envelope, the sense of animated stasis, is never broken. An emotional tableau is held in suspension, its quality of address seeming to emanate from an altered consciousness. The music stays within itself, an effect abetted by the pervasive repetition at different levels of arcs and waves, gentle oscillations. An overarching *Gestalt* takes shape from these smaller motions: one exquisitely sustained wave that builds to the high G-sharp in the soprano and then recedes. And the chords that both interrupt and enable the resolution onto this crest form the secret inner sound of the trio, the lingering "sweet sorrow" of its parting.

With examples like these in our ears, it is not hard to understand why Mozart's music is often described as if it exists in a singular state of grace. This condition is usually equated with musical perfection, or near perfection. Thus Maynard Solomon suggests in his biography of Mozart that "what may be most unusual in [some of the superlatively beautiful passages in Mozart] is their wholeness, their encapsulated sense of completion, their inherent resistance to forward motion because they have already approached a state of perfection."[5] Novelist Hermann Hesse, in the voice of his character Harry Haller, the Steppenwolf, elevates Mozart above all other composers: "[All other] music, no matter how beautiful, has something fragmentary, something dissolute about it; since *Don Giovanni*, works so perfectly cast have no longer been made by human hands."[6] And the theologian Karl Barth goes even further, when he wistfully asks: "Could it be that the characteristic basic 'sound' of . . . Mozart—not to be confused with the sound of any other—is in fact the primal sound of music absolutely?"[7] To entertain such a view is perforce to regard all other musics as corrupt, fallen—exiled from Mozart's timeless grace.

Originary perfection is somehow made incarnate in Mozart's music. It is difficult to imagine applying such a metaphorical fantasy to any other Western composer. What accounts for this? And can one do more than simply assert this sense of perfection? Solomon begins to go beyond unquestioning assertion when he speaks of an "inherent resistance to forward motion," and an "encapsulated sense of completion." These qualities relate to the sense of stasis and apartness experienced in the examples we have encountered so far: something inherent resists moving forward, moving out of the magic circle; the rapt envelope is an encapsulating wrap, the music within needing nothing beyond itself. This harks back to the original definition of perfection as describing the state of being fully made and thus finished—as though Mozart's music leaves no room for countervailing forces but rather creates and consumes all the available energy at once. But such "zero sum" perfection doesn't account for what

Barth elsewhere calls the "amiability" of Mozart's music, or what Solomon refers to as "the excruciating surplus quality" of Mozart's beauty.[8] The stasis is charged, enjoys a special burnish, a glow, a warmth: this music is not untouchably perfect but humanly scaled with ingratiating energy. Perhaps the perception of welcoming goodness, unalloyed benevolence, unstinting generosity lures us into the language of divinity—the divine at its most approachable; not just a forgiving, but a giving, divinity.

So what gives? What constitutes the pleasing emanation of these passages? Here, as in Mozart's instrumentation generally, every part has a satisfying musical role; every part *sounds*. It is almost impossible to find any of those awkward "service" parts that fill out the sound but which no one would ever want to hear or play in isolation. This is one of the reasons that Mozart's music is never labored but always buoyant. Imagine an architecture in which every buttress flies. The ingratiating self-sufficiency of each part is crucial to the overall transparency and glow. And yet this is not a world of independent contrapuntal lines—the aesthetic value here is not one of autonomous individual strands creating a discursive weave, not the enforced polyphonic identity of equalized agents. (Though when this latter sort of polyphony arises in Mozart, it often creates its own specially charged stasis, in which the periodicity of homophonic phrasing recedes and the texture becomes instantly electric.) Rather Mozart's parts are at once more autonomous and less so: they each have different kinds of roles—the melody, the sustaining tone, the punctuating bass line, the flowing middle voices—that stand out from each other and yet are pleasing in relation to the rest.[9] The result is a sonic community in which every member glows with health. Such music gives energy back to its performers.[10]

Line and Expressivity

One of Mozart's most gratifying openings is that of his Symphony in A Major, K. 201: several differentiated parts work together to transform a simple kind of linear motion into an unforgettable scene. The first violins ascend, in deliberate two-bar steps, from A to B to C-sharp to D—and then move quickly back down, retaking the entire space in less than two bars. But the combination of dropping octaves that initiate each station of the ascent and chattering repeated notes that mark the continuation of each station gives the line a distinctive character that contrasts with the half notes in the other voices. And letting the second violins also get into the business of octave leaps (bars 4–6), but on a different temporal plane, gives the entire passage a genial sound, a loosely woven heterophony, a gently intensifying ascent.

Example 1.3 Symphony 29 in A Major, K. 201, i, bars 1–9

These second violin octaves are swoops rather than the staked out, punctuating octaves of the first violins. Together they create a culminating dissonance in the fifth bar, where both upper voices move up, then down, to a dissonant second. Here the melody has reached the third scale degree and could easily have summoned a return to tonic; Mozart instead makes this the moment of greatest dissonance and then plunges forward with his chromatically ascending bass line. The entire opening phrase can be divided into two-bar units, but it doesn't come off as a conventional 4 + 4 phrase but rather as a slow climb through seven bars and a quick descent through two. This is because its progress is regulated not by the customary *devoirs* of homophonic phrasing but by the unfolding of a contrapuntal progression in the outer voices. As soon as the bass line reaches its upper limit, the A in bar 8, it drops into the most standard of cadential formulas. The long paced ascent of these three string parts creates a pleasing intertwining of lines, while the plain brusque energy of the cadence quickly discharges what had been so exquisitely deliberate in the gathering.

In his 1753 treatise *The Analysis of Beauty*, the English artist William Hogarth spoke of "pleasing turns and intertwistings of the lines" as a criterion of visual beauty.[11] Foundational to his analysis are two ideal types of line: a line of beauty and a line of grace. Hogarth's line of beauty is waving, flame-like, "composed of two curves contrasting" (see figure 1.1). His line of grace is winding, serpentine; it combines a twisting motion with the waving motion, and Hogarth illustrates it with a cornucopia (see figure 1.2).

The human form is Hogarth's most consuming study, and is taken from the inside out. Bones are invested with graceful curves. Musculature displays the aforementioned "pleasing turns and intertwistings of the lines" and is thus potentially beautiful (figure 1.3).[12] Moreover, "these exquisite turns are to be found, in some degree of beauty or other, all over the whole surface of the body and limbs."[13] To set an ideal human form in motion is to elevate Beauty to the level of Grace.[14] When Hogarth discusses Fitness and Proportion, he correlates quality of motion directly with beauty: the ability to move with grace and variety indicates the degree of beauty among animal species. Humans are best able to move in this way, according to Hogarth, and thus their forms are "superior in beauty." And "he who is most exquisitely proportion'd is most capable of exquisite movements, such as ease and *grace in deportment*, or in dancing."[15]

The perception of "ease and grace in deportment" brings us back to all those charmed characterizations of Mozart's music. Though Hogarth himself decried simplistic analogies between the arts, his lines of beauty and grace share with the Mozartean textures we have been listening to a quality of gentle undulation. Beauty of visual line and of musical texture can thus be suggested by undulation. Moreover, just as Hogarth imagines lines that do not quite express the ideal degree of wavelike undulation (he represents this ideal with line 4 in his figure 49—see figure 1.4 above), so might we be able to imagine various degrees of musical undulation that would go too far, or not far enough.[16]

Melodies also can be said to undulate, and melody is the musical element most readily analogous to a drawn line, as noted by Rousseau in his *Essai sur l'origine des langues*.[17] One of the more astonishing vocal passages in Mozart's sacred music is the result of a simple undulation. It occurs in the "Christe eleison" section of the Kyrie from his Mass in C Minor, K. 427 (example 1.4). On paper, what happens in bars 38–42 of the solo soprano's part is unassuming stuff: she traces a fully diatonic, straightforward arc over a simple harmonic circuit. And yet the result feels extravagant, like a frisson of ecstasy. The whole notes in the first two bars are like a staging area, the soprano's long, low tones gathering energy for the unfettered steps to come. The arc itself is launched in the third bar, a parabola whose peak coincides with the most colorful harmony yet in the phrase. This matching of a subdominant functioning harmony (ii^7) with the peak of a melodic arc creates a simple enough

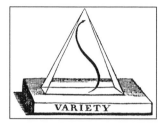

Figure 1.1. Hogarth's line of beauty encased in a pyramid. © The British Library Board. Reprinted from Hogarth, William. *The Analysis of Beauty.* New Haven: Yale University Press, 1997.

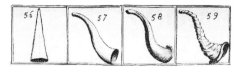

Figure 1.2. Transforming a cone into a graceful object. © The Trustees of the British Museum. Reprinted from Hogarth, William. *The Analysis of Beauty.* New Haven: Yale University Press, 1997.

Figure 1.3. Bone and muscle. © The Trustees of the British Museum. Reprinted from Hogarth, William. *The Analysis of Beauty.* New Haven: Yale University Press, 1997.

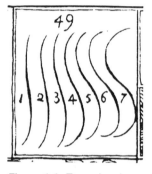

Figure 1.4. Toward and away from the ideal line of beauty. © The Trustees of the British Museum. Reprinted from Hogarth, William. *The Analysis of Beauty.* New Haven: Yale University Press, 1997.

conjunction, and yet both are marked as unique events within the phrase—together they allow the phrase its enchanted effect of approaching, passing through, and receding from an expressive high point that is also a weightless transit point between rise and fall: a simple, graceful gesture, ravishing in its execution. Unbelievably enough, the soprano then sings yet another arc, at an even higher level of intensity (bars 44–46). It is always a shock to encounter such voluptuous music in the context of a sacred Kyrie. But it is even more shocking to be ravished by a vocal gesture that in the naïve purity of its linear course is so paradoxically innocent.[18] This combination of sensuous motion and innocent bearing suggests an ironic state of being that is both artless and knowing.

Graceful melodic motion need not be limited to such overt forms of undulation. Take the oboe line that so captivated Salieri in Peter Shaffer's *Amadeus*, near the opening of the Adagio from the Serenade for Twelve Winds and String Bass, K. 361 (bars 4–5 of example 1.5).

Example 1.4 Mass in C Minor, K. 427, Kyrie, bars 38–46

Example 1.5 Serenade for Twelve Winds and String Bass, K. 361, iii, bars 1–11

Example 1.5 (*Cont.*)

Example 1.5 (*Cont.*)

Example 1.5 (*Cont.*)

Over the pulsating accompaniment, whose synchronized puffs speak with the pneumatic enunciation of a calliope, the oboe's first sustained tone sounds to rare advantage. Thus even before the oboe moves off its first pitch, its voice is marked as a kind of grace. The rest of its line is similarly gratifying. In terms of net motion, the oboe simply descends an octave. But to trace the course of that graceful descent is to learn something about beauty in motion. A long held B-flat changes color at the change of harmony, vibrant with the paradoxical stable instability of a sustained dominant with descent in its destiny. Then it begins to descend, with quick notes at the very end of the measure, its course held up for a moment with an expressive passing tone on the ensuing downbeat. As if caught by a breeze, the line is then gently impelled into an accelerating flourish with motion first up, then decisively down. Thus it partakes of an almost physical motion, like a gently gliding thing—hearing it is like watching a leaf drawn along its never-to-be-replicated drift to the ground. The oboe's course undergoes a finely calibrated kinesis, in which its final descent is given more energy, more motivation to descend by the brief rise from D to F. Not only can the line now conclude with the full force of a descending fifth, but the prevailing descent of the entire line is relieved with just enough ascending motion to make its final descent fresher, more forceful.

What follows? A diverse succession of different woodwind voices, opening up space with variously styled onsets but similarly concluding descents. The answering clarinet's increased agitation reflects the chromatically rising downbeats in the bass beneath. Its brief ascent, made expressive with trill and chroma,[19] then issues into an octave descent relieved only momentarily by another trill. The clarinet thus varies the oboe's descent. And by reaching down to the G, a third below the end point of the oboe's line, the clarinet also creates a gradual downward expansion. With the swooping basset horn, a third kind of utterance takes the stage. One would strain to characterize this line as graceful in any conventional melodic sense, but its leaps create a fresh choreography, a stunning foil to the stepwise oboe and clarinet, but also to the newly stepwise bass beneath it. The basset horn's initial octave leap (a distillation of the graceful octave descents just experienced?) is then amplified with a breathtaking series of even larger leaps into and out of a husky lower register (octave and a fourth, then two octaves and a third, then two octaves). Perhaps more striking than these staggering leaps is the strong resolution from D to E-flat in that lower register, the only stepwise move so far for the basset horn. And then its final utterance gathers up the oboe and clarinet lines and completes the collective downward expansion all the way to the tonic, resolving the melodic and harmonic process that began with the oboe's bewitching B-flat.

Thus do these voices keep company with one another, each giving what it can in graceful relay, as though engaged in a kind of *jeu d'esprit*, in which the goal is to match grace with grace, and not to touch down until the harmonic circuit is finally completed. After the cadential resolution, and as a kind of *envoi* to the entire opening paragraph, each of the voices sends up a little Roman candle, ratifying the cadence so happily attained. The oboe is granted the last word.

The opening bars of Mozart's final piano concerto, K. 595 in B-flat Major, could hardly be more different from those of the Wind Serenade's Adagio, and to hear them now may seem like trading poetry for prose. Instead of a deliciously suspended cadential progression, we hear three much briefer progressions, while the first violins occupy themselves with melodic elaborations of the tonic triad. But Mozart moves gracefully even with this blocky stage property, achieving an intensifying expressivity the more remarkable for being composed of banal materials.

After one bar of tonic introduction, the first of three melodic phrases begins with the first violins calmly ascending through the triad, as if introducing it by name. They then descend over the next three bars via turn

Example 1.6 Piano Concerto 27 in B-flat Major, K. 595, i, bars 1–13

Example 1.6 (*Cont.*)

figures on each of the notes of the triad (the last turn figure is clipped rhythmically to form a cadence). The upper note of the first two turn figures begins a stepwise descent of a fourth, to the next degree of the tonic triad. Thus the line moves back down to B-flat with a staggered series of descents, making for a pleasantly extended negotiation of a straightforward staircase of five steps. This increased amount of stepping around disguises the slower pacing of the actual melodic triad, which ascends in half notes and descends in whole notes (see level A of example 1.7). The entire phrase plays over a prolonged tonic harmony, which yields for one beat only to the cadential dominant in bar 5. Winds punctuate with a two-bar figure, descending through the triad from 1 through 5 to 3.

Then in a three-bar, foreshortened phrase, violins hop quickly up through the triad (trading half notes for eighth notes) and dally with the

Example 1.6 (*Cont.*)

F, performing a slow turn around it over two bars that then resolves through the E-flat to D. The supporting harmonies form the cadential progression ii–V$^6_5$–I; thus this phrase couples a stronger harmonic move to tonic with a weaker melodic move (5–4–3). Winds punctuate with a two-bar figure, descending through the triad from 1 through 5 to 3.

And then comes a phrase that seems to tie the first two phrases together, as a kind of trumping précis: the melody now runs its triad up to the high B-flat and then descends in two stages, each combining a triadic descent and a turn figure, answering the second phrase by means of the selfsame turn figure and similar surface rhythms, answering the first phrase by expanding its descent through the tonic triad and spinning off faster, more local triadic descents in the process. The cadential progression in this final phrase is the strongest yet, with a full bar of dominant root (F) in the bass, decorated by its neighbors G and E-flat (in yet another kind of turn figure). Thus the opening phrase becomes progres-

Example 1.6 (*Cont.*)

sively intensified with straightforward melodic means; each successive phrase accelerates on the path up the triad, from walking up, to hopping up, to running up; and each phrase further develops the idea of the turn figure. The unchanging wind interjections provide the kind of foil—including contrast of timbre (winds for strings), melodic shape (the triad now descends), and expressive quality (clipped rhythm rather than singing line)—that allows each successive string phrase to sound that much more lyrical and expansive.[20]

It is wonderfully instructive to see how Mozart varies this entire opening line when the piano enters (example 1.8): he now enlivens each phrase with more notes, increasing the number of turn figures and finding opportunities for expansive runs. Had Mozart written his own *Analysis of Beauty*, this example could serve as an illustration of how to animate a melodic line and still maintain "graceful deportment."[21]

Example 1.7 Progressive generation of melody from background

Example 1.8 Piano Concerto 27 in B-flat Major, K. 595, i, bars 81–92 (piano part only)

The opening of this concerto brings to mind Rosen's memorable assessment of Mozart's melodic shapes, which "are rarely as idiosyncratic as Haydn's. . . . Mozart needed his motifs to sound ordinary; it allowed him to release the latent expressiveness in the tonal language with ease, so that moments of concentrated energy could act as a shock."[22] A potent expressive shock of this sort may be heard at the outset of the Adagio from the Piano Sonata in F Major, K. 332. The first two beats of the melody make a graceful, if ordinary move: the opening B-flat rises to its third scale degree D, elaborated with a turn figure and seemingly poised to ascend to F. But this innocent business of ornamentation is instantly transformed into breathtaking expressivity on the very next beat. It is not the E-natural itself, a common enough chroma attending the fifth scale degree F, but rather the triple accent of the E—metric (on a strong beat)

Example 1.9 Piano Sonata in F Major, K. 332, ii, bars 1–2

and agogic (greatly extended in duration) and contextual (appearing at the change of bass and harmony)—that shocks the decorum of the phrase. It is as though a single fleeting ornament suddenly becomes imposing enough to pull the entire phrase into itself. As when seized with a sudden surge of anguish or desire that floods our consciousness at the barest reminder of an absent beloved, we are reminded of what seethes beneath the surface, how emotional energy can gather in strength, and at once. The melodic material that precedes the E is ordinary, but its decorative friction builds static electricity, which Mozart chooses to amplify and release all at once. The shock of the E is compounded by dropping to the C so quickly after the arrival on F. With an ornament as striking as that E-natural, we might expect an F of even greater extent. Instead, the phrase ends as though to point up the gratuitous extravagance of its climactic expressive gambit.

The effects of the E reach beyond the bar into the next melodic phrase, which answers handsomely. The opening E-flat of this phrase does many things at once: it sounds as the freshest possible note to follow in the wake of the extended E-natural; in conjunction with the subdominant harmony it neutralizes the pull of the E-natural toward the dominant side of the key with a nudge toward the flat side of the key; and it allows Mozart to parallel the span of his first phrase by giving him another fifth through which to ascend. Thus he is permitted to spin yet another gorgeous length of melody, with a matching expressive shock at the end. So now there are two luxuriating spans, both warmed with turn figures, both voluptuously expressive. And we are only two bars into a long opening period!

In terms of expressivity, the opening of this Adagio is exceptionally eventful. But even Mozart's calmest, least troubled melodies can harbor dissonant notes that gather and concentrate expressive force. Take the melody from the slow movement of the Piano Concerto No. 21 in C Major, K. 467, in which a triadic line finds a telling dissonance. What could be more at ease with itself than this opening, especially the first three bars? That famous melody: consider its calm yet swelling rise through the triad F–A–C, the energy for each new rise of a third coming

Example 1.10 Piano Concerto 21 in C Major, K. 467, ii, bars 1–23

from double-dotted-rhythm rebounds and culminating with a long stay on the high C. This triadic figure is forecast by the bass line, which simply spells it out while the same triad pulses *con sordino* in the other strings. Mozart's melody brings this basic figure to expressive life, as if transforming it from ground to voice. He thus performs a fundamental move of homophony—namely, the transference of harmony to melody. This saturation of the F-major triad works to profile what follows. The long C descends on the last beat of the bar through four sixteenth notes back to F, traversing by step the space so elegantly opened up through the triad. But there's no resting on that F. An arresting *volte face* turns the melody back upward a crucial half step, from the would-be point of maximum stability to a highly expressive chroma (F-sharp, the sharp-1 scale degree), which endures for a long beat on its way to the second scale degree. The phrase is then answered by a more straightforward ar-

Example 1.10 *(Cont.)*

Example 1.10 *(Cont.)*

peggiation of the dominant seventh (without dotted rhythms), followed by another downward stretch in eighth notes (rather than sixteenths) that also swerves into an upward chroma (sharp 2), on its way to the third, A. Both of the dissonant notes occur at the change of harmony and inflect tones in the new harmony—they are thus coupled with a change of parameter, helping to mark harmonic boundaries. Sharp-1 marks the turn to the dominant; in the next phrase, now on the dominant, sharp-2 marks the return to tonic.

After these two phrases, the melody indulges in huge registral swoops: C–A–B-flat, with C as appoggiatura; then D–B-natural–C. The A and the B-natural function somewhat like the earlier dissonant notes, for they ascend as leading tones to the next harmony. A hidden chromatic line emerges from the composite of all these "leading" tones: F–F-sharp–

Example 1.10 (*Cont.*)

G–G-sharp–A–B-flat–B-natural–C. This line of course fills in the original leaping figure from F to C. There is a logic operating here; dissonance creates an expressive rhythm, actuates and motivates a lengthy linear process through expressive hinge points (yearning chromatic ascents, to be precise). For all its expansive elegance, Mozart's melody is instinct with expressive dissonance.[23]

The concentrated expressivity of line we have been listening for helps inflect the sense of "amiable perfection" adumbrated earlier. Graceful motion couples with expressive pangs, as in the "yearning chromatic ascents" I choose to hear in the Andante theme from K. 467. It is not uncommon to describe some of these effects with the language of physical pleasure, especially when a chromatic note creates an isolated frisson within a generally diatonic context. Again think of the Andante from the concerto: a relaxed, triadic melody embeds a chromatic note that is accented in such a way as to deliver a small shock of pleasure. Such plea-

Example 1.10 (*Cont.*)

sures are not isolated to chromatic touches within melodies. Sonority it-self is also described in this way, as when Charles Rosen speaks of the "physical delight" to be taken in Mozart's "sensuous play of sonority, and indulgence in the most luscious harmonic sequences."[24]

To bring this way of taking in Mozart's music to the often prevailing sense that his music is "untouched by human hands" is to be faced with a kind of untouchable music that is deeply touching. Ideal grace merges with real sensuousness. This kind of merger troubles the notion of perfection so often implied in accounts of Mozart's music. In a context such as the opera *Don Giovanni*, the stakes are raised. The above remark of Rosen's arises within his discussion of *Don Giovanni*, where he associates Mozart's music with erotic seduction:

Perhaps no composer used the seductive physical power of music with the intensity and the range of Mozart. The flesh is corrupt and corrupting. Behind Kierkegaard's essay on *Don Giovanni* stands the idea that music is a sin: it seems fundamentally sound that he should have chosen Mozart as the most sinful composer of all. What is most extraordinary about Mozart's style is the combination of physical delight—a sensuous play of sonority, and indulgence in the most luscious harmonic sequences—with a purity and economy of line and form that render the seduction all the more efficient.[25]

In Rosen's view, the result of such a merger is potently subversive art: Mozart corrupts sentimental values by rendering his "supreme expressions of suffering and terror . . . shockingly voluptuous."[26] Nor is Rosen alone in letting Mozart unsettle his own perceived perfection. "Trouble in Paradise" is the title of one of Maynard Solomon's chapters on the beautiful on Mozart, and in a later chapter he discusses "[t]he strange, the terrible, the uncanny, and the deadly aspects of beauty" in Mozart's music.[27] To bring this perception of Mozart's art into sharper focus, we need to hear him stage some encounters with the extraordinary, to listen for traces of the supernatural, the demonic, the divine, or the deeply personal. At issue will be the special ability of Mozart's music to intimate the preternatural, lingering at the threshold of the distant sublime, or of the deeply interior, or of both at once, as though to invite us to feel the intimacy of awe, the inward bruise of the beyond.

THRESHOLDS

Summoning the Supernatural and the Sacred

Of the countless articulations that mark our lives, there are some few that remind us of our place among larger rhythms. In the face of these we are stilled with a sense of something greater than us, something that transcends the quotidian. Time adjusts accordingly.

When Giovanni fatally wounds the Commendatore in the opening scene of Mozart's *Don Giovanni*, the turbulent music of their struggle suddenly gives way to a music of suspended animation (example 2.1). Mozart creates the stunned reaction to the Commendatore's death out of the headlong immediacy of dramatic commotion. At its height, Giovanni's fatal thrust pierces the Commendatore on an alarmed fermata, a diminished-seventh sonority from the nether side of the dominant of F minor (bar 175). This stroke culminates a staged fight, choreographed by the composer with upward lunges and rhythmic sword clashes. These almost mechanical gestures are supported upon a harmonic sequence that carries the opponents from Giovanni's cadence in D minor downward to A, then G, then F, and further to a first-inversion B-flat sonority (A, D$^6_5$, G, C$^6_5$, F, B-flat^6). At this point the harmony changes course, and the upper line that has been descending bar by bar turns around, accelerating into the dominant of F minor and beyond, into Giovanni's *coup de damnation* on the diminished-seventh chord, a musical exclamation mark.

Everything changes after the fermata. The overheated thirty-second-note runs are gone; the sforzandi, gone; the downward stomping bass line, the harmonic aggression, all gone. In the hush of their absence, the awestruck trio of Giovanni, Leporello, and the dying Commendatore remains in place, singing lines that now seem to float within a new temporality. Pizzicato lower strings mark a slow pulse; violins run in place with triadic triplets—these small details sound with etched hyperreality,

Example 2.1 *Don Giovanni*, Act 1, Scene 1, bars 163–94

imprinted the way mundane details are when you hear the news that changes everything.[1] A pedal point on the dominant of F minor holds things still.

Each character reacts in his own way, with his own style of line. But Giovanni's reaction is the most overtly lyrical, perhaps because he alone observes, while the others are busy communing with their own conditions. His is thus the overriding consciousness of the scene. Leporello's stunned exclamations (twice mouthing the fatal diminished seventh) give way to his usual trembling patter. The dying Commendatore is reduced to gasps, his sustained A-natural in bar 187 a final flare of vitality before the last breath. This pitch carries the sound of tragic irony, brightly lifting

Example 2.1 (*Cont.*)

Example 2.1 (*Cont.*)

away from F minor only to move upward into a subdominant trafficking morbidly with G-flats. After the Commendatore dies into the cadence, sinking half steps trace lines of somber destiny. They pass through the A-natural again but this time take it down through the A-flat rather than upward to the subdominant. The B-natural in the line is also drawn down, forgetting its usual upward move to the dominant. Thus the reflexes of life fall slack.

But the overall effect of this passage is not one of crushing anguish. There is no overbearing pathos here, nothing so heavy. Rather what meets the ear is a light, hovering texture. This lightness is a key to the experience. It constitutes what Mozart understood better than most. We

Example 2.1 (*Cont.*)

have the rest of our days to measure and bear the full weight of a momentous revelation. But the revelation itself dispels the gravity of the mundane. Mozart allows us a liminal experience, by placing us on the threshold of the supernatural.

If the Commendatore's death brings on the supernatural as the sudden absence of overbearing sound, the very beginning of the opera's overture achieves a related effect with the sudden onset of such sound (example 2.2). For many listeners, the opening of this overture (bars 1–4) is one of the great shockers of the Viennese Classical era, right up there with the beginning of Beethoven's *Eroica*. The harmony textbook is no help here, for it instructs us only that we hear a tonic followed by a dominant, as in any number of declamatory symphonic openings. It's probably a given

Example 2.1 *(Cont.)*

Example 2.1 *(Cont.)*

that a loud tonic *minor* at the beginning will always be arresting, but
beyond that, how could such everyday ingredients create the effect of this
opening, which is not just arresting but materializes with paralyzing immediacy, like the head of Medusa?[2]

As always, the scoring tells. We hear brass on the stentorian octaves D
and A; winds on the full chords; upper strings syncopating against the
basses' implacable half notes, the last of which sustains beyond the upper
voices. This single beat of remaining sound is the most frightening touch
of all: to hear the bass emerge like this is to feel the menace, to realize
that the terrifying face is looking at *you*.[3]

The half-step motion of the bass line is also crucial to the overall effect. Deploying the leading tone at the bottom of the dominant chord

Example 2.1 (*Cont.*)

allows the fifth in the strings to work its own stark horror, while avoid-ing a parallel octave with the upper voice. The first inversion also makes for a less stable form of the dominant, which in turn attenuates the more standard effect of regal declamation of tonic and dominant. We hear the frightening mobility of power rather than the reassuring stabil-ity of power.

What follows is an insinuating echo of the opening, letting its enor-mity seep in slowly, quietly: beginning in bar 5, the winds twice repeat the D and A, now in descending octaves, while the lower strings present a slow chromatic descent to the dominant in dotted rhythms, ominous in their steadiness. When the pedal point on the dominant arrives in bar 11, anxiety mounts, with syncopated first violins quickly joined by the ner-

Example 2.2 *Don Giovanni*, Overture, bars 1–39

Example 2.2 (*Cont.*)

vous sixteenth-note patter, Leporello-like, of the second violins. Striking harmonies ensue, in a more melodramatic styling—and then comes the extraordinary passage beginning at bar 23, which combines the dotted rhythms of bars 5–10 in the bass with the nervous sixteenth notes in the first violins. The harmonic progression alone is an effective example of tension-raising chromaticism, as each half step moves further from the brass pedal point on D. Trumpets and drums mark that D on each down-beat, not for ceremonial pomp, but rather as the sound of immovable

Example 2.2 (*Cont.*)

fate. The D disappears only at the remarkable arrival of the E-flat chord in second inversion in bar 27. This has a clarifying effect at first (in that it clears the D out of the system while stopping the violin runs), then turns out to be only the advance staging of an augmented-sixth arrival on the dominant of D minor. But what makes this entire passage unforgettable are those violin scales—moving up then down, rising in half steps along with the bass and winds. Who would have thought to profile this drama of rising half steps against an interior pedal by filling each chromatic step with the banal utterance of an ascending or descending scale? And yet the effect is stunning. As though in a stupor, the violinists

Example 2.2 (*Cont.*)

Example 2.2 (*Cont.*)

seem reduced to moving their fingers unconsciously, capable only of marking the rising half steps sounding around them on a kind of abacus of fear. This combination of unusual chromatic harmonies with the most common imaginable melodic pattern feels uncanny. Here again, we are faced with the hair-raising effect of liminal experience.

That first chilling step from D to E-flat which begins this chromatic ascent is echoed in the Molto Allegro, now as the sound of growing excitement, rising from D through D-sharp to E in the first violins. This move may also be heard as mockery of that frightening half step. After

Example 2.2 (*Cont.*)

all, mockery of the fear of consequences is a leading trait of the Liber-
tine; such jibes are the jangling spurs of his bravado. Don Giovanni
raises these stakes, for he makes *music* of the fears of others, which may
be what makes him the most charismatic of all the Don Juan incarna-
tions. But that shared half step also reminds us that Giovanni's merri-
ment is borrowed from perdition. There's an edgy boisterousness to this
Allegro celebration, a simmering violence, as in those oft-recurring
downward thrusts, many of which outline a tritone (e.g., bars 77 and
following). We are not permitted to forget what stands behind it all:

Example 2.2 (*Cont.*)

Example 2.2 (*Cont.*)

those sovereign chords of the opening, the once and future sound of abject damnation.

Don Giovanni wishes to live in a clamorous series of Nows, as though to shut out the sound of the past and future.[4] But when past and future disappear, their reappearance—as embedded within the supratemporal realm of the Commendatore—is that much more momentous. Mozart's opera stages this juxtaposition of supernatural time and human time, stages the boundary between Giovanni's Now (his No to past and future), and the Commendatore's Always. In the first-act death scene, we

Example 2.2 (*Cont.*)

heard a fiercely Now moment cross over into a timeless moment. Similar crossings haunt this opera, which is made vivid by our abiding fascination—at times fearful, at time awestruck—with the supernatural, and with transgression. Transgression materializes the supernatural. Giovanni is the lightning rod that both mesmerizes the other human characters and draws down the taboo energy of ageless terror. The bolt strikes in the second-act finale, but its premonitory static electricity first prickles the air in those uncanny violin scales of the overture.

A much safer way to summon the supernatural is through the act of prayer. Mozart stages the act of prayer in the Confutatis movement of his Requiem, at the text "Oro supplex et acclinis, cor contritum quasi cinis,

Example 2.2 (*Cont.*)

Example 2.2 (*Cont.*)

gere curam mei finis" (I pray, bowed and kneeling, my heart contrite, ashen: have a care for my end). The passage is remarkable in both its local and overall motions. It begins by shifting into a different realm (example 2.3). When the bass line reenters the musical texture at bar 25, after eight bars of women's voices in suave counterpoint, it quietly pulses underneath a sustained harmony that is spelled out by a reiterating string rhythm. The chords change slowly, bar by bar, as the strings climb up and down in hypnotic undulation, tracing the gradual sinking of tonal stations in a mysterious harmonic sequence. After the initial A-minor

Example 2.2 *(Cont.)*

sonority, we hear solemn cadences on A-flat minor, then G minor, then F. The descent is made possible at each stage by the transformation of an already striking chromatic move into something extraordinary.

Among the notable chromatic maneuvers of this period is the transformation of a diminished-seventh sonority to a so-called "dominant-seventh" sonority. In this transaction, a fluid and dissonant sound transforms to a more stable chord, and indeed, a chord that all by itself can indicate a key center (no other sonority is quite as able to pull this off). What makes the move singularly effective is the fact that it can be done with the absolute minimum of motion: one voice simply descends by a half step. (Any of the four voices of the diminished-seventh chord can do

Example 2.2 (*Cont.*)

this, with the result that four different dominant sevenths, four different key centers, are available—hence the value of the diminished seventh as a tonal solvent, a sonority that can dissolve a key center and transform it into another one.) Here in the Confutatis prayer, Mozart employs a series of metamorphoses from diminished seventh to dominant seventh. But instead of the simple move of allowing one tone to descend a half step, Mozart holds one tone steady and asks the other three tones to *ascend* by a half step. The harmonic result is essentially the same—a diminished seventh is transformed into a dominant seventh—but the effect is full of mystery. Moreover, the stable note is in the bass each time, with the effect that the world rises around it, along with a concomitant effect of sinking, the way that motion around us will often induce a sensation of our own

Example 2.3 *Requiem*, K. 626, Confutatis, bars 25–40

motion in the opposite direction. This mysterious transaction happens
four times. To begin the first three of these, the instrumental bass leaps
downward by a tritone from a tonic root, landing in an unrooted sonority. After this precarious leap into the void, the bass then persists while
the world moves around it, transforming it into the stable root of a local
dominant. (The third iteration of this pattern is foreshortened, dropping

Example 2.3 (*Cont.*)

Example 2.3 (*Cont.*)

directly to the C rather than cadencing on G-flat minor, in analogy with the first two iterations.)

This sense of the world moving around a subject held still is the uncanny "through the looking glass" side of normative reality, in which a subject moves through the world. The motion-without-motion brought on

Example 2.3 (*Cont.*)

each time the diminished seventh lifts off the stilled bass note also takes place at the level of the entire descending sequence. Remember that the entire tableau sinks by half steps, each of the uncanny motions taking place a half step lower than the last. This happens because a diminished-seventh chord that is normally treated as a vii°7/V resolves, instead of to V of that key, to V of the key a half-step lower. The sharp 4 of the old key becomes the 5 of the new key. Thus the same move that makes the bass feel as though he's sinking when he's really sitting still also makes it possible for the entire passage to sink while seeming to sit still. Moreover, we are made to feel as though the operative piece of harmonic mystery transpires within each key, as opposed to doing so between one key and the next. This is due partially to the fact that the chromatic shift happens at the level of the dominant rather than the tonic (how banal and obvious it would be to juxtapose independent, self-standing cadential phrases in A minor, A-flat minor, and G minor). In addition, the diminished-seventh sonority that follows each successive tonic preserves enharmonically two tones of that tonic (e.g., A-flat minor becomes G-sharp diminished seventh, with A-flat becoming G-sharp and C-flat becoming B); this gives the bass tritone the effect of a leap into some as yet uncharted inner space. The entire passage thus takes on the aspect of continually sinking inward.

With this in mind, we may return to the textual context of the passage: prayer. And not just any prayer: this is the prayer of prayers, undertaken within the psychological space of mourning, asking for nothing

Example 2.4 Handel, Funeral Anthem, HWV 264, opening chorus, bars 1–17

less than eternal salvation, warding off nothing less than eternal damnation. Mozart's music matches the stakes of this prayer, by staging a hushed mystical interface with the divine.[5]

Mozart's Requiem establishes its special atmosphere at once, with the very first sounds of the Introitus—so much so, that it is astonishing to discover that Mozart modeled a number of the salient aspects of this opening movement on a Handel funeral anthem.[6] The comparison is revealing, for it shows what Mozart was inclined to add to his model.

The Handel anthem opens with harmonies whose temporal spacing (each harmony is insulated by rests before and after) gives the impression of a stately procession. When the oboes and violins enter with a brief imitative figure, their sustained notes are like voices of lament heard over this austere funeral march. Mozart deploys similar harmonies but allows

Example 2.5 Mozart, *Requiem*, K. 626, Introitus

them to sound on the backbeats, giving the bass line more prominence
and enlivening the rhythm. He also brings in sustained bassoons and basset horns right away, with successive imitative entrances of the same melodic figure (borrowed from the opening vocal line of Handel's anthem).
Their mid-register blend is a kind of sonic thumbprint of Mozart's music

Example 2.5 *(Cont.)*

Example 2.5 *(Cont.)*

from this final period. In conjunction with the organ, they provide the characteristic sound of the Introitus: richly shadowed, removed from the world, yet not ominous. The effect is much like stepping from the light of day into a cathedral.

Example 2.5 *(Cont.)*

Once again the ancient compact is revealed, and all else falls away. This is not the stunned stasis of the awestruck individual (as after the Commendatore's death) but rather the enveloping and shared aura of solemn ritual. And yet even this shuns the usual invitation to be lugubri-ous and instead remains buoyant—the various harmonic turns argue for

Example 2.5 (*Cont.*)

Example 2.5 (*Cont.*)

mobility, for a lighter tread, even, in the case of the turn to C major in bar 5, for a poignant sweetness. And the backbeat chordal texture lightens what would be a trudging rhythm—we step not with heavy chords on

Example 2.5 *(Cont.)*

our backs but with the bass line under our feet. This rhythmic texture also sets off the sustained basset-horn voices, which essentially (at first) double lines in the strings, or, better, provide voice-like versions of the string contour. The punctuated string contour is thus made liquid, with transporting effect. A ritual disposition is created by the antique contra-

Example 2.5 (*Cont.*)

Example 2.5 (*Cont.*)

puntal rhetoric of imitation at the fifth. As has been noted by Christoph Wolff and others, Mozart makes reference to older models of religious music in his Requiem, lending his own style a new solemnity. But the lightness remains.

Example 2.5 *(Cont.)*

Trombones mark the entrance of the voices with three upbeat quarter notes, as though heralding the entrance of the priests, reminding us once again of the special role of trombones in sacred music, the thrill of their dusky grandeur. Trumpets and drums join on the last upbeat, and now the majesty of Death is upon us, with instantaneous effect. Strings are

Example 2.5 *(Cont.)*

animated, keening, like a turba in distress;[7] winds meld with the voices; and voices solemnly call out for what the winds quietly requested from the outset: "Requiem aeternam dona eis" ("Grant them eternal rest"). The now shortened interval between vocal entrances intensifies both the texture and the urgency of the plea. This seething mass of voices crests on the soprano F before sinking along the ritual descending tetrachord to the dominant.

But the bass then continues to descend two more steps into bar 15, effecting a rapid modulation to F major, whose transformation to the dominant of B-flat major colors the text "et lux perpetua luceat eis" ("and may perpetual light shine upon them"). Thus a heavy dominant arrival in D minor falls away into light—Mozart uses its own descending momentum to make the change. But the best is yet to come. "Et lux perpetua" rings out twice, with regal bearing; and then "luceat eis"—"may it shine on them"—sounds with a warm infusion of harmony, full of burgeoning possibility, as the line crests on a G. This half-diminished seventh chord has a special lightness: dissonant yet expansive, promising a renewed tonal focus with oblique suggestion, much like the grammatical force of the subjunctive mood in the verb "luceat." (In more prosaic terms, the chord is the next stage of intensification of the dominant sonority prolonged through these bars, which begins as a simple V on the first "et lux perpetua," moves to a V^7 on the next, and tops off with an incomplete V⁹ on "luceat.") The setting of "luceat eis" stands out as a deft example of Mozart's fluid expressivity, how he finds fresh emotional energy (a swelling of hope) within a prolonged chord waiting to be resolved. And that chord's immediate resolution onto a first-inversion B-flat still maintains the buoyancy of a yet-to-be-fulfilled hopeful thought.

When the cadence finally does drop in bar 19, after a fleeting inflection of minor (a flickering qualm?), it initiates a new section with a new text: "Te decet hymnus, Deus" ("For you, O God, a hymn is fitting"). As though taking refuge in B-flat major, the music finds itself in a lyrical oasis, with flowing sixteenth notes moving like fresh streams around the tender declamation of a solo soprano.[8] The fact that she sings a chorale-like phrase only enhances the perceived degree of personal subjectivity.[9] But this moment of personal song cannot last. Already with her second phrase, the soprano slides back into minor (G minor this time), where she is reabsorbed into the full chorus singing "Exaudi orationem meam" amid an austere swarm of dotted rhythms. When the "requiem aeternam" music returns in the D minor of the opening, the words "dona eis" ("grant unto them") are now irrigated with the sinuous lyrical streams from the "Te decet." This infusion of the warm breath of lyricism into the space of ritual expression reveals the personal, even familial, relation toward the deity at the heart of Baroque Catholic sensibility.[10]

The parts of the Requiem that Mozart completed himself continue to develop the dramatic dualism of ritual and personal. After the forbidding majesty of the Rex tremendae, the Recordare takes place wholly within the sphere of the personal plea ("Remember, merciful Jesus, that I am the cause of your journey"). Lyrical basset horns are again crucial to the atmosphere but now create a very different effect from that of the Introitus. Technically in canon at the second, they conjoin in a slow stepwise ascent, circling around each other in alternation, meeting in dissonance at each downbeat. The underlying pattern, a rising chain of 2–3 suspensions, is an old one. Robert Gjerdingen identifies it as a "Corelli leap-frog," and it serves as an effective engine for linear ascent.[11] But leap-frogs are among the very last things that would come to mind in the presence of such gracefully styled sound. Instead we hear two voices gently pulling each other up in companionable poignancy. The result is a beautifully braided line, made even more precious by the ministrations of the cellos, whose second beats (from bars 2 to 5) create yet another ascent (C–D–E–F). The separate components of this lower line—its initial scalar descent, and its trill figures—then join together over a pedal point on the dominant (adding basses), with the violins now ascending in canon. But this is again achieved without a trace of academicism; rather the effect is of a sweet proliferation of diatonic sound, drifting up from each pulse of the pedal C like clouds of incense.

Example 2.6 *Requiem*, Recordare, bars 1–14

The duality of exterior and interior, impersonal ritual and personal plea, is staged most dramatically in the following Confutatis. Its opening, a churning portrayal of the damned consigned to the flames, departs categorically from the pious charms of the Recordare. But this initial music is far from the whole story; in fact, it sets only the first clause of the first sentence of the text: "Confutatis maledictis, flammis acribus addictis" ("The damned being silenced, consigned to acrid flames . . ."). We are hanging fire (in more ways than one) within an ablative absolute construction, a dependent clause. The downbeat of the sentence is its next clause: "voca me cum benedictis" ("call me among the blessed"). This

Example 2.7 *Requiem*, Confutatis, bars 1–10

text thus hands Mozart the opportunity to oppose damnation and salvation directly, and he meets the challenge. His setting of "voca me cum
benedictis" is different in every way from the "flammis acribus" of the
opening. Over string lines echoing those in the Recordare, we hear sustained vocal imploring, women's voices only. In fact, Mozart deploys the
genders in Confutatis as if separating animus and anima, in a kind of
psychic titration, the male principle shouting downward amid the din of
damnation, the female floating up like Goethe's *ewig Weibliche*.[12] The

Example 2.7 *(Cont.)*

movement concludes with the "Oro supplex et acclinis," the prayer like no other.

Mozart breaks up the long text of the requiem Sequence into separate numbers, which until the Confutatis alternate in character between impersonally imposed fear and personally kindled hope. The frenzied Dies irae is answered by the calmer Tuba mirum, the imposing Rex tremendae by the sweetly pleading Recordare. And then the Confutatis concentrates and combines this charged contrast. The oscillation of character is an artifact of the Requiem text, to be sure, but one that Mozart the dramatist stages unforgettably. As in *Don Giovanni*, the music again creates a threshold for the supernatural, is haunted by the same specter of Death and Damnation. But while the opera is rapidly speeding toward the spectacle of damnation, the Requiem's dramatic oscillations have the effect of deepening into a timeless plea for salvation. As a work left incomplete at the very end of Mozart's life, the Requiem stands forever at the threshold, its freight of hope and fear balanced in an eternal moment.

With this in mind, the ascending crescendo in the Lacrymosa, often thought to be Mozart's final finished phrase, becomes almost unbearably significant.[13] It can be heard to gather all the preceding emotional energy into one consummate motion. We ascend, rising through harmonic layers of hopeful color, rising still into harsher light, into the glare of the judgment to come, and upward still, onto the home dominant of the entire Requiem.

Example 2.8 *Requiem*, Lacrymosa, bars 5–8

Mozart went no further. As for us, we may well drop from the zenith of this dominant back into the beginning of the Introitus, as though to cycle forever through these sacred scenes, as though to complete the Requiem ourselves, to make it endlessly whole.

The motet *Ave verum corpus*, composed in the first month of Mozart's final summer, seems to dwell entirely within the condition of *Ahnung*, of intimation. Its hushed strings and four-part chorus create a warming nimbus, and this special envelope of sound sustains from first to last. Part of this effect is due to a blend of churchly and personal musics, again as though the supernatural and the natural—or, in the motet's liturgical context, Christ and the communicant—meet and merge at a shared threshold. Alfred Einstein hears "ecclesiastic and personal elements flow together" and goes on to proclaim that, with this motet, "the problem of [Mozart's sacred] style is solved."[14] The urge to hear such rapt music find its highest calling in the solution to a compositional problem is not uncommon in music-historical reckonings. However one chooses to fit the motet into the multifarious stream of Mozart's church music, I would like to dwell here on its effect of sustaining a self-contained liminal state of divine presentiment, and on what it feels like to move around in such a state.

Ave: the gentle expressive warmth of this word builds the sonic ethos of the motet, which can be heard as an extended projection of this benevolent greeting. The first choral "Ave" is already beautiful, emerging from the transparent glow of D major with graceful triadic leaps in the

Example 2.9 *Ave verum corpus*, K. 618

Example 2.9 *(Cont.)*

Example 2.9 (*Cont.*)

Example 2.9 (*Cont.*)

Example 2.9 (*Cont.*)

Example 2.9 (*Cont.*)

soprano; the second "ave" brings on a transfixed dissonance, as blessed-ness develops to awe. This sonority—D, B, E, A—has a delicate bell-like ring; it could be opened outward into a resonant stack of fifths (D, A, E, B), but it remains contained, a fleeting touch.[15] The A suspends the G of a ii$_2^4$ chord, which it reaches chromatically via G-sharp. The use of a ii$_2^4$ creates a sense of liftoff from the tonic. It makes the bass itself dissonant (such that the bass must resolve down to the leading tone underneath a V^6 or V$_3^6$), and this can have the effect of a momentary decentering, so often the prelude to insight. Mozart compounds the inherent effect of the ii$_2^4$ with the suspended A that rings above. The chromatic move that follows (A—G-sharp—G) is an emblematic reminder of the suffering of Christ that will be expounded in the phrases to come, while the negation of G-sharp's usual urge to move back up to A is as a small, sweet act of personal resignation.[16] We will hear the soprano's leap to D two more times in the motet, on the fraught words "cruce" and "mortis"; here it is but a *praegustatum*. Much has transpired in this quietly devout opening phrase: wrapped in a holy nimbus, we have heard a churchly bell-like resonance, the lift of awed presentiment, and the close chromatic bite of personal emotion. Sweetly svelte thirds in soprano and alto close this phrase and then continue through the next four bars. These thirds will also return, to usher in the final station of the ritual.

The text "Ave verum corpus" is a Eucharist hymn, designed to accompany the ritual of Communion. In this ritual, specially blessed wine and wafers are said to undergo a mystical transubstantiation into the blood and body of Christ. Thus the text of the hymn asks for Christ to serve us as a foretaste of heaven in the trial of death, or more broadly, a foretaste of redemption within the toils of mortality. As though to fit the magically compressed dimensions of the communion host (the small unleavened wafer that is placed by the priest on the communicant's tongue), the hymn text presents a compact version of the fate of Christ's body: hail true body, miraculous body (born of a virgin), suffering body (immolated on the cross, with flowing wounds), dying body, redeeming body.[17]

In the second phrase, on the text "vere passum, immolatum in cruce pro homine," the soprano A again moves down to G-sharp, but this time the G-sharp persists, as the phrase heads into A major. The accented syllable of "immolatum" pitches even further into the sharp side of things, as an E-sharp inflects an F-sharp minor triad. It is from the local context of this latter sonority that the soprano leaps again from A to a now lonely D, for the phrase "in cruce." The drama here is understated, as though to keep its voice down, and yet this very reserve beckons us to attend to every gesture. Christ on the cross: this central—literally and figuratively crucial—image is portrayed here with a single tone, as by a finger's touch at the center of the phrase. We will hear this isolated sound only once again, as a kind of rhyming moment in the final vocal phrase, for the words "in mortis."

If the second phrase tends toward the sharp side of D major, the third phrase finds the flat side. To mark the beginning of this process, the soprano's A now moves to B-flat, in an inverted response to the move from A to G-sharp in the previous phrase. But the full shift into flat-side space is reserved for the word "perforatum." This reference to the wounding of Christ's side sounds with a wondrous move into an unsuspected realm: wondrous because the taut diminished seventh sonority is heard to relax, with the tiniest but most telling shift, as the tenor's C-sharp slackens into a C-natural, to which the bass answers with a rooted C. The piercing of Christ's mortal envelope is thus heard as a release. But no sooner does the C dominant seventh resolve onto F major, then another harmonic mystery follows, with the word "unda" ("with water"). Here the F in the bass is decentered, transformed from stable root of a briefly tonicized F major to very unstable seventh of a G dominant-seventh sonority. This sonority does not go on to tonicize C major but rather finds the diminished seventh on C-sharp from a few bars ago and moves through it to D minor. The progress toward this end was foreordained by the first move from A as tonic to the diminished seventh rooted on C-sharp. But the harmonic move into and out of F gives the middle of this phrase a miraculous turn inward, a glance toward that same mystical space of the "oro supplex" prayer from the Requiem.[18]

Congruent with its overall emphasis on the flat side, the entire third phrase flows downward toward the half cadence from which the final choral phrase will emerge. Thus the sharp-side rise into the dominant key of A major is now balanced with a flat-side declivity that reestablishes A major as the dominant of D. Moreover, the D-minor coloring at the end of the third phrase makes the major-mode luminosity that ensues almost unbearably special.

One more phrase of the text remains, the burden of the entire hymn: "be for us a foretaste (of heaven) in the trial of death." In keeping with the imperative "esto," the soprano F-sharp at the beginning of the final section marks a determined new beginning. The imitative texture that follows separates the women and men into two strands of thirds. This has the effect of creating a slow alternating step, as in a ritual procession. And the overall motion is upward, with the sopranos regaining the A that began most of the other phrases. There is a labored aspect to this motion: not only are third-strands texturally heavier than individual lines, but the overall sequential pattern of downbeat dissonance doesn't glide downward with 7–6–7–6 but rather pulls itself upward with 7–8–7–8 (the sevenths resolve locally to sixths but this is in the service of the larger pattern). Or perhaps this rising motion is not so much labored as deliberate, as would befit the dignified elevation of the host. However construed, this act of elevation could easily and effectively bring on the final vocal cadence of the motet. All lines of text have been set, and a full cadence on D would fulfill the tonal contract: half cadence, full cadence in V; half cadence, full cadence in I. And indeed, after the ritual stepwise procession brings the sopranos to their A, they linger there for over a bar and then move as though to a definitive cadence, dropping through F-sharp to E (over a cadential six-four–five-three formula). But at the last moment they turn the line back upwards, to G, while the basses nudge their dominant A up a step to B. The result is a breathtaking turn to the subdominant in first inversion. Students of harmony will classify this move as a type of deceptive cadence, and like that conventional figure this too suddenly creates space for a new phrase out of the expectation of an ending. But the effect is vastly different. Rather than bringing the old phrase up short with a rooted vi (which is like landing on the tonic but with the wrong foot), Mozart's IV[6] opens the phrase outward, warms it with a breath of mystery.

This sets the stage for what will prove to be a kind of denouement for the motet, a breakthrough, transformative moment. The words "in mortis examine" return (this is the only text repetition in the motet); the sopranos leap once again to an isolated D, as they did with "in cruce." But here the D *rises*, through D-sharp to E, touching the highest point of the vocal line and then descending in a sinuous line that includes one more leap to D, perhaps as a last memory of all those other D's. Most spectacular of all is the stunning enharmonic effect of a D-sharp in a local harmonic context of G minor that would seem to call for an E-flat. The slightly sharper cast of this note, as it ascends to E, gives this moment a fleeting sense of harmonic destabilization, a tremor of confusion, as the passage of death takes us from the flat side to the sharp side of D major. Thus the harmonic areas contrasted in the second and third phrases, the two phrases that encompass the suffering of Christ, are mystically conjoined in one harmonic metamorphosis. The bass line succinctly marks this crossing from flats to sharps with chromatic neighbors surrounding the dominant A: B-flat to A to G-sharp. And then the G-sharp lets go, loosening into G rather than rising back up to A. This move is part of a slow chromatic descent in the bass from B-flat to F-sharp, the longest chromatic line in the motet. The F-sharp supports the soprano's last upward leap to D. After this, all is cadence. The passage as a whole captures the exalted sense of being in the presence of death, not as a constricting terror but as an ennobling expansion of experience.

The string postlude that closes the motet is inexpressibly poignant. On the one hand, it is nothing more than cadential convention. And yet, as its appointed dissonances move into consonant resolution, it becomes nothing less than the paradox of suffering and blessedness rendered in one figure of finality. Within the precincts of this motet, even the most constrained conventions of tonal language are made to sound miraculous.

The mysteries of *Ave verum corpus* are embodied in subtle gestures, the various stations of its drama signaled by the smallest shifts: A to G-sharp, then E-sharp to F-sharp in the second phrase; A to B-flat, then C-sharp to C in the third phrase. Most broadly telling of all is the way that the sopranos' opening A to G-sharp to G, an inwardly resigned gesture, is transfigured in inversion with the climactic D to D-sharp to E. In this way the motet moves from the inwardly personal to the outwardly transformative.[19] None of these profoundly consequential gestures ever pierce the sonorous envelope, the holy nimbus. Mozart stages the great Christian mystery of corporeal pain and spiritual redemption as a ravishing, yet quietly personal, revelation. Within the world of *Ave verum corpus*, the word of God is a whisper in your ear, a rustle in your blood, a breath.

Pandemonium

After music granted such a hushed audience with the divine, it will be bracing to face another kind of supernatural intervention in Mozart, revealed in passages that are decidedly more demonic. As in the transfixed passages from the sacred works, these too lift off from the prevailing character of the music, these too leave us open to awe—but they do so by bursting out of the frame of the music with sudden, searing energy.

We encounter such an eruption at the very heart of Mozart's Piano Sonata in A Minor, K. 310. The sonata begins and ends with turbulent, even violent, Allegros. Poised between them, the F-major Andante breathes a different air, as its opening makes abundantly clear.

Example 2.10 Piano Sonata in A minor, K. 310, ii, bars 1–8

Space opens up and contracts with relaxed plasticity in the first phrase, and the ensuing themes are warmed by an elaborative, variational impulse—plenty of lambent energy flickers throughout.

The development section begins with a new theme, square-cut and supported by dense block chords in a lower register (example 2.11).[20] At bar 37, the music slips into C minor as into a darkly moving stream; the quietly running triplet arpeggios in the left hand liquefy the bluff chords of the preceding bars. Things are underway. A rising sequence moves us forward, then a prolonged augmented sixth grows into a loud arrival on the V of vi (bar 43).

Suddenly the air is electric: instant, riveting intensity, as the triplets now jump into the right hand. Repeated pitches galvanize the relentless rhythm, while syncopated, poking octaves make them dangerous, like whipcracks. Helping the effect is the double resolution of the augmented sixth sonority that precedes this bar. Both B-flat and G-sharp resolve to A (at different temporal levels)—no other harmonic resolution can potentially load so much energy onto one pitch class. And then this turbocharged A is drawn into an extended contrapuntal progression: it collides with a B-flat that pushes it down as the first move in a seven-bar chain of 2–3 suspensions (taking into account the right hand only). The dissonant seconds in this chain are wildly multiplied in the rapid repeating rhythms of the right hand, maximizing their energy. Mozart maintains the level of excitement throughout by varying the harmonic resolutions (now by fifth, now by linear motion) underneath the 2–3 braid and also by adding even more textural commotion with the left-hand trills. Rarely has a contrapuntal sequence been staged with such naked power. This "perfect storm" takes three and a half bars to subside, during which the dangerous triplets drop back into the bass, neutralized into the safer activity of a dominant pedal point.

Example 2.11 Piano Sonata in A minor, K. 310, ii, bars 32–53

Example 2.11 (*Cont.*)

Example 2.11 (*Cont.*)

A similar eruption occurs in the C-minor Fantasia, K. 475, as a quietly portentous harmonic question is answered with a sudden swarm of thirty-second notes.

Example 2.12 C-minor Fantasia, K. 475, bars 129–38

Example 2.12 (*Cont.*)

As in the passage from the earlier sonata, this turbulent effusion is sustained by a contrapuntal descent in the right hand, initially profiled in the upper register and fantastically extended: the opening high B-flat descends over two octaves, burning through a vivid diversity of suspensions and resolutions.

Both these passages burst forth with Dionysian frenzy, as though seized with a sudden access of preternatural energy. Dissonance drives them both, the most elemental kind of contrapuntal dissonance, staged with maximum intensity. Each passage seems to gather and discharge the electricity of all the music leading up to it, and each leads (directly in the case of the sonata, indirectly in that of the fantasia) to the return of the main theme. These are localized disturbances. In the sonata, we may even talk of the storm before the calm, a process that allows the ensuing theme an even rarer beauty.[21] But concentrated dissonance and matchless beauty, though they may enhance each other through contrast, are never straightforwardly opposed in Mozart's music.

Beautiful Dissonance

Dissonance in Mozart is rarely routine; and though it is often breathtakingly extreme, it is never ugly or shrill. We can test this notion by judging the effects of some of Mozart's harshest simultaneities. Arnold Schoenberg will help get us started. After all, Schoenberg knew a few things about dissonance, having "emancipated" it, as the most pervasive accounts of Western music history and Schoenberg himself like to claim. As part of his brief for dissonance, Schoenberg was on the lookout for extraordinarily harsh dissonances in the music of earlier composers. And he was well served by Mozart; he finds what on paper is a staggering dissonance in the first movement of the G-minor Symphony, K. 550 (bar 150).[22]

Example 2.13 from Schoenberg *Harmonielehre* (Vienna: Universal Edition, 1922), figure 233, p. 392

The shock of Schoenberg's example (at letter a) is mitigated somewhat when he provides the context for it (at letter b). Here we see that the dissonance is an artifact of the appoggiatura structure, part of the sighing motive that saturates the movement. But this is not just any appoggiatura. Mozart creates a kind of hyper-appoggiatura, by combining a descending appoggiatura figure with an ascending appoggiatura: E-flat and G resolve down to D and F-sharp; G-sharp and B resolve up to A and C. Melodic sighs are themselves appoggiaturas, but this dissonance performs a pitch multiplication almost in the Boulezian sense, one that would result in a bitingly dissonant stab of anguish, an effect as bold as anything in the *Eroica* Symphony—except for the fact that it is played softly and goes by quickly (see winds in bars 150, 152).

Example 2.14 Symphony 40 in G Minor, K. 550, i, bars 147–52

The effect of this is so fleeting that one hears it not even as a dissonance but as a slight disturbance in the air, an aural smudge, something akin to the non-pitch noise some instruments make when heard close up.

But there exists in Mozart a symphonic dissonance quite literally as bold as the *Eroica*'s most famous dissonance, and it is found in the slow introduction to Symphony No. 39. After an exquisitely wrought sequence over a pulsing pedal point on the dominant B-flat (bars 9–14), the B-flat and its insistent rhythm switch to the upper registers (bar 14). This has the intensifying effect of bringing the action closer. A new rising sequence begins, in which the operative dissonances sound in the pulsing upper voices. B-flat dissonates with A-flat, as a V[7] of E-flat; two bars later a C piles onto the B-flat, as a V[7] of F minor. And suddenly D-flat is on C, with loud flutes adding to the clash of upper-register violins. This bar is powerful not just because of that nakedly scored clash. Mozart also foreshortens the harmonic rhythm here (one would reasonably expect an

Example 2.15 Symphony 39 in E-flat Major, K. 543, i, bars 9–25

entire bar of F minor), while also switching dynamics instantly from piano to forte, while also pitching the music toward the subdominant, from which Mozart launches one of his most mysteriously wonderful cadences.

In material terms, the dissonant chord in bar 18 of Mozart's introduction is the same as the well-known dissonance from the middle of the first movement of Beethoven's *Eroica*: a "major seventh chord" in first inversion, with the half step on high, in the harshest possible scoring (example 2.16). Although Beethoven's dissonance (starting in bar 276) is an exact transposition of Mozart's, it does not arise as the hottest link of a linear sequence but rather as an astonishing *non plus ultra*, a showstopping dissonance after which the scene must change. Beethoven's disso-

Example 2.15 (*Cont.*)

Example 2.15 (*Cont.*)

nances in the *Eroica* seem to precipitate themselves more as verticalities, and they can come on with the visceral force of blows; Mozart's are always more linear, as in the heightened sigh, or other types of tragic intensification. (Of course, Beethoven's famous dissonance can also be analyzed linearly, as a kind of Neapolitan harmony about to resolve to the dominant of E minor. But the lines of resolution are disguised through registral isolation, such that the A–C–E–F sonority sounds like a shriek overriding the expressive repertoire of any given individual, as though the earth itself were raising a cry.)

But Mozart can also precipitate sonorities that are not just dissonant but outlandishly foreign sounding, as though from another language. In

Example 2.15 (*Cont.*)

the Andante cantabile from the Piano Sonata in B-flat Major, K. 333, the first section repeats by turning down a lane that leads right back to the tonic E-flat and the voicing of the opening theme (example 2.17a). But when we return to that lane and cross the double bar line into the second section of the movement (example 2.17b), we encounter a sound so different as to make us question our own ears. This example is shocking because of what we are trained to expect by the piece (and by tonal music). The contrary motion between the hands at the end of bar 31, so obviously headed for a tonic, is pulled up short in each hand. For a moment, our tonal gyroscopes are knocked out of commission—the sound is so foreign as to be hard to process (imagine biting into a cherry cordial and tasting goat cheese). At the second beat of this bar the strange sound resolves: into one of the least stable sonorities in Mozart's vocabulary!

Example 2.15 (*Cont.*)

Example 2.15 (*Cont.*)

And when this sonority would seem to resolve in turn, by being grounded with a C in the bass that suggests the dominant of F minor, the C moves up to D-flat, prolonging the tension. And the next bar after this brings yet another expressively dissonant downbeat, and the next as well. The entire passage writhes with the dissonant energy unleashed by that alien sound, only settling into F minor on the second beat of bar 35.

The dissonance from the G-minor Symphony is a musical sigh "in extremis" that precipitates and dissipates in an instant; the passage from the E-flat-Major Symphony is a shriekingly scored but grammatically unexceptional dissonance that arises as the high point of a contrapuntal sequence. And the dissonance from K. 333 is a shocking grimace that results from a contraction of linear motion. Mozart's staging of this latter

Example 2.15 *(Cont.)*

sound further reveals the boldness of his treatment of dissonance, the sense that he can get away with anything. But we will hear him raise the stakes still higher.

In the middle of the Andante of the Piano Sonata in F Major, K. 533, we come across a passage remarkable both for the stridency of its dissonance and for the sheer length of time such dissonance is sustained (example 2.18). The passage will eventually lead back to the return of the main theme (at bar 73), but when it arises, it comes on with the force of an irruption. In a long ascending sequence, the upper voices consistently clash with the left hand on the downbeats but do so with sonorities that are themselves consonant—first sixths, then thirds. This circumstance, coupled with the registral span between the hands, lends the passage a sound of ringing plangency, especially in the three bars with the sixths

Example 2.15 *(Cont.)*

(60–62). And then thirds clash against sevenths on the downbeats of the next two bars (63–64). Finally, thirds clash against thirds, as both hands continue the ascending sequence by mobilizing phalanxes of thirds (as if each outer voice were now a sonority, an interval class, rather than a single pitch). Each of these stages increases the amount of dissonance on the downbeats: comparing the downbeats of 60, 63, and 65, we register an increase of seconds, from one to two to three. Moreover, the underlying contrapuntal progression is in effect a *rising* chain of 2–3 suspensions: the initial G that enters against the left hand's F in bar 60 does not push the F down; rather, the F scoops up to G and then the G in the upper voice leaps up to A, and so on. By thus withholding the normative falling resolutions of dissonant progressions, the passage increases its dissonant energy. But—and this is extraordinary—at no point in this

Example 2.16 Beethoven, *Eroica* Symphony, Op. 55, i, bars 272–84

process do the combined sounds cease to ring sonorously. We hear sixths against octaves, then thirds against sevenths, then thirds against thirds. The effect of these shifts is kaleidoscopic rather than monochromatically harsh, complexly resonant rather than just noisy.

Finally, the extent of the ascending sequence is remarkable—a full twelve bars. The pianist Malcolm Bilson once pointed out to me that the passage is also unusual because it is so unrelieved: no pauses, no empty spaces, no breathing room—he referred to it as "a breathless taffy pull."[23] Remarkable as well is the reach of the passage: once the right-hand thirds commence in bar 62 they ascend from B-flat–D all the way up the octave

Example 2.16 *(Cont.)*

and beyond to C–E-flat, positioned as the top third of the home key's dominant seventh. The high E-flat then tumbles through a five-octave arpeggiation, discharging the energy of that dissonant climb in which every step was contested, in which one hand must traverse by step what the other hand has just leapt, until the contrary motion in bar 70 signals the end of the process. To return to the quiet originary thirds of the opening theme after this roiling string of thirds is to hear something like the echo of the crashing of hell in the bite of an apple.

And what about that opening theme? Does it give any clue of the storm to come? The opening ten bars of the Andante (recapitulated ex-

Example 2.17 Piano Sonata in B-flat Major, K. 333, ii, (a) bars 29–31, then bars 1–4 (first ending into return of tonic); followed by (b) bars 32–35

Example 2.18 Piano Sonata in F Major, K. 533, ii, bars 59–82

actly in bars 73–82) in fact constitute a study in the poetics of dissonance. After an innocuous sounding first bar that blends a passing motion in thirds in the left hand with a melodic neighbor motion in the
right, the outer voices leap down in parallel sixths across the bar line,
such that D–B-flat descends to G–E-natural. (Because these are two different sized sixths, the leaps are different: the bass descends a perfect
fifth, the soprano a tritone.) This is an astonishing move. A standard
voice-leading gambit is followed by a leaping collapse in all three voices
to a dissonant, nondiatonic sonority.[24] The dangling live wire that is the
E-natural then swings up to a C rather than resolving up a step to F, a
daring move that somehow resolves the collapse into a yet higher position than the opening sonority.

The next phrase continues the longer-range melodic motion from B-
flat (bar 73) to C (bar 74) by offering a sustained D followed by a quick
E-flat (bars 76–77) and then a sustained F (bars 78–79), eventuating in a
chain of appoggiaturas that ladder up to a high C on the downbeat of
bar 81. The line then moves down by local steps, recovering that long-
lost E natural, and cadencing via one more appoggiatura onto the dominant F in bar 82. The ascending action here brings to mind the middle
section, with its unmitigated contrapuntal ascent. Also like the middle
section, the ascent in the second phrase of the opening theme (from the
upbeat to bar 77 on) pushes forward with ringing dissonances on the
downbeats, even unto some of the selfsame sonorities. The right-hand
dyads held over the bar lines into bars 77 and 79 create progressively
more dissonance (the sixth F–D over the C proceeds two bars later to the
more dissonant third D–F over the E-flat). This progression of dissonance
is precisely what gets amplified with such vehemence in the grinding dissonant skein in the middle of the movement. And there is more dissonance to come before the theme reaches its cadence on the dominant:
each beat of bars 80 and 81 seems to get more dissonant. Bar 81 contains
the registral climax of the theme and three beats of free-falling dissonance: C over the G (with a D), A over the G (with a B-flat), then F over
the G (with C and B-flat). These clashes are sharply profiled because of
the daring leaps down in the inner voice (again the leap down to a dissonance!).[25] The dissonant plenitude of the entire passage is gathered
into the triple appoggiatura that begins bar 82, the culminating dissonance before the varied repetition of the theme.

In both the opening theme and the passage before the return of that
theme, we hear a labored ascent attended by ringing dissonance, in fact
all kinds of dissonance—a veritable glossary of dissonance, of clashing
blends. Mozart's control of such varying degrees of dissonance, his exacting deployment of dissonance as a progressively calibrated expressive element, brings about an extraordinary turn: we begin to hear dissonance

as an aesthetic presence that goes beyond the simple binary of consonance and non-consonance, becoming more like a quality of atmosphere, which precipitates with greater or lesser concentration.

If the Andante of K. 533 offers striking stretches of dissonant saturation, the Minuet for piano K. 576b seems entirely founded on outrageous dissonance. It relates to more normative dance movements of the period as cubist painting relates to conventional portraiture.

The three loud augmented chords in the A section stand out like cymbal crashes. But the very opening of the minuet is even more strikingly odd. In fact, if you play the first two bars slowly and deliberately you will hear a series of sonic solecisms—after the first sonority, only one of the

Example 2.19 Minuet in D Major, K. 576b

Example 2.19 (*Cont.*)

subsequent verticalities in these bars is consonant (the fleeting E–E–G-sharp). And, moreover, these verticalities move awkwardly from one to the other. D moves to D-sharp in the left hand at the same time that the F-sharp–A dyad moves to G–B in the right. Then, when the D-sharp moves to E, the upper voices move back down to F-sharp–A! What's more, these voices continue to descend not to the consonant E–G but rather to the dissonating E-sharp–G-sharp. When they finally reach E–G, the bass has moved on to C-sharp followed by A.

What saves this awkward succession of sonorities is the coherence of the upper and lower parts in and of themselves. These lines comport as though in different dimensions; they are slightly out of phase. The upper voices begin and end a beat earlier than the lower voice. There is a symmetrical chromaticism that helps stabilize the action: the bass line's chromatic ascent from D to E is answered by the upper voice in thirds, now descending from A–F-sharp to G–E. The passage displays Mozart's deft sense of the framing power of tonic and dominant, their ability to contain such outlandish sounds.

The opening may be heard as a knowing distortion of a more "acceptable" sequential pattern.

Example 2.20 Recomposed opening of K. 576b

My recomposition profiles the strangeness of Mozart's second sonority (D-sharp, G, B). This fleeting augmented triad is an artifact of the parallel voice leading, and it will go on to haunt the A section. Counting this swift apparition, the A section in fact presents all four possible augmented triads. As in the Andante from K. 533, we encounter a kind of saturation of sonic alterity.[26]

On a first hearing, the dissonance at the opening of the B section of K. 576b (bar 17) is so sharp as to sound like a mistake (in fact, I like to imagine Mozart falling into the keys here, as a result of being vigorously clapped on the back by his pal Schikaneder, and then making music of the mishap). As with the marked augmented triads in the A section, we hear a loud dissonance drain off to resolution. But the crash of *this* dissonance strips away all pretense of decorum—it is almost unheard of to front-load a phrase with this much dissonance. Its explosion marks the onset of two different descending motions: the marching descent of the quarter-note dyads and the slow drifting descent of the dotted half notes. Add to this the skittering descent of the sixteenth notes, and the result is a counterpoint of different temporal motions.

That aloof chromatic span in dotted half notes prompts us to rehear the A section as permeated with chromatic spans. These include the opening left-hand figure and the answering right-hand figure; the ascending thirds in bar 3; the middle-voice ascents spawned by the loud augmented chords in bars 5, 7 and 9; and the answering descents in the upper voice in bars 6, 8, and 10 (these last contain some intervening notes but clearly outline chromatic descents). The C–B–B-flat–A span at the outset of the B section also figures in Mozart's recomposition of the opening as it returns later in the B section: the move from C to B in bar 29 is answered a bar later by B-flat to A. Moreover, another short chromatic span is introduced across the bar line, as D-sharp moves through D to C-sharp. To hear this span comport with the C–B–B-flat–A span as well with as the A–G-sharp–G span in the upper voice of bar 30 is to experience the most concentrated gathering yet of chromatic segments. The richness of these bars allows Mozart to recreate the haunted otherness of his opening, to reconstitute its freshness of effect.

And finally, after all these chromatic sallies, the banal normality of the last five bars of both A and B sections sounds dissociated, brightly surreal in its insouciant disregard of all that has gone before.[27] Convention becomes Other in this out-of-phase minuet.

Out-of-phase dissonance can sound like a visitation. Mozart's single most famous dissonance is surely the first note of the first violin in the slow introduction to his String Quartet in C, K. 465, known forever afterward as the "Dissonance" Quartet.

Example 2.21 String Quartet in C Major, K. 465, i, bars 1–5

As a pitch class, the A-natural of the first violin would seem impossibly gauche, appearing as it does after the successive entrances of C, A-flat, and E-flat in the other strings. But the *mise en scène* of this impossible dissonance is utterly captivating: as if in a séance, a mysterious and solemn invocation in the lower strings summons the ghostly A-natural, a sonic apparition from on high that glides only gradually into the known, corporeal world as the upper note of a turn figure. Thus a common ornament is here made uncanny, its slow devolution signaling a different temporal dimension. It is hard to resist hearing this oblique, out-of-phase dissonance as a brush with another order of experience.[28]

The opening of the Andante from the G-minor Symphony, K. 550, stages this out-of-phase effect in a different way, by having the violins transform a line first heard in the bass. The effect is of invertible counterpoint made uncanny. The violas speak first, beginning a string of imitations, then burrowing into the middle of the resulting texture with a persistent E-flat that will be taken up by the horns in the next phrase. Basses

Example 2.22 Symphony 40 in G Minor, K. 550, ii, bars 1–12

and cellos touch E-flat and G before being drawn into a line that chromatically circles the dominant as though in a trance, providing an inspired foil to the talismanic repeated eighth notes above. The imitative
process begins again with the pickup to bar 9, but now the bass figure
from the first phrase is transfigured in the first violins, as if released into
a new time scale that floats above the rest of the texture. The violins'
slow ascent, in even dotted quarters, in registral isolation, stretching an
already dissonant A-flat to A-natural and then taking that preternatural
step to C-flat, as though into a dimension beyond: here the former bass
line grows ever more entranced, as with eyes held open, as if drawn mysteriously upward before resolving, finally, to the dominant B-flat. Again

the music brushes a threshold, the path to its appointed cadence merging for a long moment with a path from some other time, some other space.

In the midst of the bewitching minor-mode interpolation to the famous theme from the Andante of the Piano Concerto in C Major, K. 467, another such visitation occurs (see example 1.10, bars 11–19). Several different orbits are launched in this passage, chief among them the lines traced by first violins and second violins (doubled by bassoon). At the downbeat of bar 15, these orbits graze each other in such a way as to generate a remarkable combination of pitches: from the bass up we hear C, B, F, B-flat, A-flat. The wide-open spacing of this sonority attenuates the fact that it contains a cluster of pitch classes a half step apart (C, B, B-flat). If you were to take this sonority out of its context here and remove the B-flat, you would hear a fairly common configuration: a vii^7 over a tonic pedal. But by retaining the B-flat as a cross relation to the B-natural at the same time that B-natural is sounding against the C, Mozart has transformed and elevated a common dissonant configuration into something *unerhört*, something even more dissonant and yet strangely beautiful, mournfully sonorous. The previous downbeats work up to this extraordinary sound, each with an increasingly haunted dissonance (in 12 we hear C^7 with suspended F and D-flat; in 13, F minor over C in the bass, with suspended G; in 14, C^7 with suspended D-flat and A-flat).[29] After the otherworldly dissonance materializes in bar 15, the lights are brought up gradually, the ghosts dissipated.

An even more extraordinary example of uniquely Mozartean dissonance can be heard in the slow movement of his viola quintet in E-flat major, K. 614 (example 2.23a). In bar 79, within a lengthy middle section in E-flat, the untroubled gavotte figure from the movement's B-flat major opening suddenly finds an astonishing dissonance (example 2.23c).

With the onset of this special dissonance, Mozart's simple gavotte now seems to be speaking in tongues. To create this effect, he introduces dissonantly juxtaposed pairs of sixths (he overlays the B-flat–G with C–A-flat). This dissonance is not easily parsed. It is not simply a combination of tonic and dominant, though it has elements of that. Nor is it an orthodox 13th chord (with added ninth), because the A-flat sounds above the G. With the C, and the juxtaposed sixths, Mozart achieves a sound both strikingly dissonant and sonorously bell-like, again as if finding a spectral resonance from some other dimension.[30]

Comparing the phrase in example 2.23c with that of example 2.23b, it becomes clear that Mozart drops two new voices onto the original pair of voices from bar 54. These new voices, in first and second violin, overlay the existing tonic-oriented strand with a dominant-oriented strand. By thus placing one harmonic function onto another, Mozart creates a

Example 2.23a String Quintet in E-flat Major, K. 614, ii, opening two phrases, bars 1–8

Example 2.23b Opening of E-flat section, bars 54—57

Example 2.23c Dissonant phrases to return of opening, bars 80–90

rare instance of synoptic temporal comprehension, a moment in which events from different points in time may be perceived together. Such a moment comes on with the force of altered consciousness. Mozart rings this uncanny bell three times in succession before bringing the action to a definitive resolution on the home dominant, prior to the return of the opening theme.

In examples like these, Mozart conjures unheard-of sounds, plaintive and yet pleasantly thrilling, strange and yet exquisite. They can all be explained as the result of linear gestures, but they maintain a stubbornly haunting presence. For this reason, they place us on a threshold of our own as listeners: we are caught up in an absorbing cognitive tension between hearing these dissonances as linear epiphenomena (and explaining them away as such) and hearing them as aesthetic phenomena in their own right (and savoring them as such).[31]

Mozartean dissonance of this special sort seems to signal a preternatural presence; it does not leave us longing for consonant resolution, nor does it leave us shattered and overwhelmed. Rather it leaves us brushed with awe. This is dissonance as intimation—as *beautiful* intimation—and it is a new kind of dissonance. It is not simply marked as the absence of consonance, as the audible need to resolve. And thus it is not primarily there to help consonance be heard as a form of resolution. Music that sets up resolution after resolution creates a ready analogue to the free and consequential exercise of reason, of decision.[32] Dissonance is the problem that gets resolved through the power of reason acting in concord with nature. This is why Classical-style music plays so well as a product of the Enlightenment.[33] The intimational dissonance we have begun to track in Mozart enjoys a rather different effect, an oblique effect, by inviting another dimension to the experience. It is not there primarily to stage the confirmation of reason; instead it complicates the Enlightenment scenario by staging some dissonance not as a problem demanding resolution but as a seductive threshold (the payoff here is more the brush with another order of experience than the resolution of a problem).

Thus we are not talking about dissonance for the sake of consonance but dissonance for the sake of dissonance. This is dissonance as a kind of *surplus*. There is an available analogy to the onset of ironic self-consciousness, for just as dissonance can be heard here as surplus, so too can self-consciousness be conceived as a surplus to simple consciousness.[34] The burr of dissonance, like the burr of consciousness, suggests an added dimension, a dimension that, in Mozart's music, beckons with strange beauty.[35]

The philosopher George Santayana closed his lectures on beauty, delivered over a century ago, with this sentence: "Beauty is a pledge of the possible conformity between the soul and nature, and consequently a ground of faith in the supremacy of the good."[36] In other words, beauty tells us we belong; the perception of beauty is a form of well-being, in which existence needs no apology. But Mozart's beautiful dissonance is a special inversion of Santayana's beauty—one that seems to answer to the ironic pain of consciousness. This is beauty through which consciousness is heard to be in exquisite disharmony with nature. The word "dissonance" itself, as a Latinate compound of the prefix *dis* and the present participle *sonans*, denotes a "sounding apart." Precisely *not* in harmony with nature but aware of standing apart from nature—this is the gift and the curse of consciousness in an age of irony, allowing us to conceive of nature as a redemptive force even while exiling us from that force.

Friedrich Schiller theorized about his age's drift toward self-conscious art in his 1796 essay "On Naïve and Sentimental Poetry." Naïve poets, such as Homer and Shakespeare, were able to represent a finite reality to perfection; sentimental poets, the moderns, attempt but imperfectly to represent an infinite reality. No longer comfortably at home in the real world, their art reaches for the ungraspable. With his beautiful dissonance, Mozart brings sentimental self-consciousness to naïve grace, intimates the ungraspable with perfectly grasped musical language. This is why Hermann Abert refused to understand Mozart as either naïve or sentimental but rather as both at the same time.[37]

And with this we touch upon the originary impulse of the modern construction of self, that point at which Enlightenment rationality creates the space for an irrational Romanticism to emerge, an individual and interior space.[38] Mozart, poised at the crossroads of the Enlightenment and Romanticism, offers ironic intimations at once revelatory and resigned, redemptive and melancholy. We hear the sound of these intimations as beautiful. The awe we experience in perceiving them is not overwhelming, not in the sublime manner. Rather we find ourselves poised again on that hair-raising threshold, poised again in that weightless place where we hear old certainties about darkness and light become disarticulated; where we hear the ironic plight of self-consciousness become an enchanted opportunity, disharmony become exquisite—and where we begin to recognize ourselves in all our twilight complexity: as both self and other, sympathetic and distanced, sincere and feigned, partaking in an expressive emotional ambience that can precipitate deep joy and deep sadness, that can suggest the promise of transcendence beyond or within.

Moving Inward

Let us return yet again to the Andante from Mozart's Piano Concerto in C major, K. 467, now putting together some passages we have considered separately (example 1.10). The orchestra introduces the movement with twenty-two bars of rapt music, held within an envelope of gently pulsing *con sordino* strings. Halfway through, this music of placid and effortless beauty takes a turn into some other realm before coming back to the business of thematic convention and closure. After a six-bar melody that moves with the ease of convention from tonic harmony to dominant harmony and back, the bass line underpins the now swooping violins with a steady chromatic ascent on the downbeats of bars 8–11. The pitches of this ascending bass (A, B-flat, B-natural, C) indicate a common approach to the dominant, with intent to cadence. But when the bass arrives on C, it persists there for the next six bars, while the harmony does not resolve the A-flat of bar 10 to an expected G or even A-natural, but holds to it over the bar line, thus seeming to enter a state of enchantment within the minor mode. The unfolding melodic period now falls away, and a different logic takes over. During the ensuing six bars, the upper voice descends on minor-mode scale degrees from D-flat to F, each step down the sum of opposed but unequal leaps. This descent is counterpoised by the more stepwise and sinuous ascent of an inner voice, sonorously scored in octaves for bassoon and second violins and marked by the dissonant suspensions on each downbeat that we noticed earlier.[39] The pedal point in the bass holds the passage in a suspended state of apartness, the upper-voice descent keeps it directed, the general rise of dissonance gives it an increasingly otherworldly sound—and then the bass finally moves off its C and steps down to A, just as the upper voice gets to F, arriving together at bar 17 on the first downbeat in quite some time that is consonant. This first-inversion tonic sonority has a limpid, daylight clarity not unlike the easing of a fever, and the music soon arrives at its appointed periodic cadence.

When the piano soloist then takes up the theme in bar 23 (example 2.24), we hear a much more normative and undisturbed 6 + 6 period (after a one-bar introductory vamp). But this would-be normality cannot mask what we heard first: the original presentation of the theme, with its center expanded and its periodic gravity suspended, with its revelation of a strange, new world emanating from within the phrase.[40] This world disturbs Mozart's beautiful surface with an even more transfixing beauty, a captivating and terrible beauty.

Mozart's music often stages passages that arise as inspired interpolations in the middle of a phrase and that seem to signal the emergence of a higher—or deeper—consciousness, passages that have been felt to brush the listener with what Rudolph Otto called "primal numinous awe."[41] Such passages may well have moved E.T.A. Hoffmann to exclaim: "Mozart leads us deep into the realm of the spirits. Dread lies all about us yet withholds its torments and becomes more an intimation of infinity."[42] In

Example 2.24 Piano Concerto 21 in C Major, K. 467, ii, bars 23–35 (piano solo)

saying this, Hoffmann was eager to claim Mozart as a Romantic artist. His reference to intimation (*Ahnung*) suggests that he recognized a liminal element in Mozart's music, a sense of being on the threshold of some other state of mind. And he often referred to this other state as the realm of the spirits.

Hoffmann's realm of the spirits is arguably the interior realm of consciousness, increasingly recognized around 1800 to hold both exalted inspirations and unspeakable terrors, transcendence and madness, a deep and uncharted space within each of us, a space fearlessly explored by the artist and cravenly shunned by the philistine. For Hoffmann, Mozart announces the first glimmers of this kind of consciousness by composing music that makes this newly conceived interior space resonate—and this is what makes Mozart a Romantic artist.

In the early twentieth century, music critic Donald Francis Tovey often referred to "purple patches" in the music of Mozart and others (usually Haydn and Schubert).[43] These purple patches are deeply colored, richly expressive passages, and they almost always involve a move into tonal regions on the flat side of the prevailing key center, the subdominant side. Moves to the sharp side of a key, the dominant side, involve an increase of tension and a sense of moving out of that key. Explorations of the flat side of a key seem rather to move within the key, to speak of its inner depths. This is partially because the flat side is the side of the minor mode, through which the major mode can be expressively enriched without even changing its key center. The parallel minor mode can thus sound as a latent expressive realm within any given major key. And because the tonic harmony can be said to contain the subdominant harmony within it, as a kind of nether projection from the tonic note, the subdominant harmony itself can be heard as a sign of interiority. (The traditional "amen" cadence is as good an illustration of this as any: while the final tonic continues to sound in the voices of the congregation, the subdominant opens up a space beneath and within that tonic, and "amen" is given the kind of musical support that allows it to arise like a ratification swelling up from deep within.)

As a classic example of a Mozartean purple patch, consider the following example from the slow movement of the G-minor Symphony. A transparent phrase in B-flat major plunges into its flat side, only to emerge in an exultant cadence. With a sudden infusion of sonority at bar

Example 2.25 Symphony 40 in G Minor, K.550, ii, bars 41–48

Example 2.25 (*Cont.*)

44, Mozart mobilizes a phalanx of flats, transforming an unpretentious phrase into something that seethes with emotion. First violins enact a drama of D-flat burrowing down to B-flat and then rising to a now luminous D-natural at the cadential six-four; outer voices slowly rise by half steps toward the same shining moment. Because this interpolation expands from the middle of the phrase, and because it has recourse to the flat side of the key center, it is made to sound as if emanating from within.

The passage from the Andante plunges into the flat side and then transfigures the ensuing major-mode key center, now profiled as something special rather than something conventional. Perhaps the most powerfully affecting example of this kind of transformation occurs in the Adagio ma non troppo of the G-minor String Quintet, K. 516. As in the Andante from K. 467 and the farewell trio from *Così fan tutte*, the strings are played with mutes, always a signal that rapt music lies ahead. The passage in example 2.26 occurs twice, once in B-flat and once in the tonic E-flat. I illustrate it in the latter (home) key, for this version enhances an already potent effect: through an extended and multidimensional exploration of the flat side of the key, the major mode returns as if transfigured.

After an airy cadence on the dominant, the scene darkens suddenly in bar 55. E-flat minor appears with a concentration of will, its sixteenth notes restlessly churning underneath three plaintive, probing descents of a seventh in the lead violin. The second viola in bars 56 then 58 answers the first two of these descents with throbbing despair. Then this somber procession is stilled as the music plunges deeper yet into the flat side, pushing through to find the rare light of C-flat major, written enharmonically in the cello as B major. As G-flats persist in the upper violin, the texture below becomes a sonic kaleidoscope, shimmer-shifting chromati-

Example 2.26 String Quintet in G Minor, K. 516, iii, bars 55–74

Example 2.26 *(Cont.)*

Example 2.26 *(Cont.)*

cally. The cello part is a guiding thread here, winding up and down before pulling into the dominant B-flat. (It is worth tracing this line, which consists of the bottommost cello notes: B, B-sharp, C-sharp, D, E-flat, D, C-sharp, C, C-flat, A, B-flat.)

Then comes the miracle. Mozart simply allows his cadence to resolve back to E-flat major, but that key and its treatment now sound impossibly poignant. The G in the first violin is placed as with the tap of a magic wand at the top of the texture through the leap of a tenth, where its warm glow transmutes the pedal G-flats just heard in that register. And now we again hear those melodic descents of a seventh from a few moments before, as well as that earlier section's active accompanimental commotion, but both are transfigured into a major-mode texture. The

Example 2.26 *(Cont.)*

relentless pulsing despair of the minor-mode texture is now aerated with off-the-beat buoyancy. When the first viola and first violin begin to sing a duet in bar 69, the piercing sweetness of their exchange is almost unbearable. The entire texture seems to smile through tears, somehow both world-weary and suffused with hope. This is an astonishing emotional effect, one that would be rivaled only by Schubert.[44]

Mozart does not always need to plunge so deeply into the flat side to achieve an effect of emotional ballast. Sometimes the diatonic subdominant harmony itself can work in this way. At the outset of the slow movement from the "Jupiter" Symphony, notice how Mozart withholds the subdominant until the second big phrase, and how the movement only finds its feet (or, rather, finds its bass line) when this harmony enters in bar 7.

Later in the movement (example 2.28), Mozart again exploits the latent expressivity of the subdominant. Some untroubled phrases in C major are followed by a circle-of-fifths progression that leads to the subdominant and the makings of a cadence. But before closing the circuit, Mozart interrupts the cadence with a repetition of the circle of fifths (bar 35). And this time around, the subdominant (F) finds its own subdominant (B-flat) with a two-stage bass descent by thirds (from F through D to B-flat). The effect is one of taking increasingly deeper breaths, filling an increasingly expansive inner space—and then the bass line climbs back, step by step, into the daylight of C major.

Mozart never reaches for these effects; like much else in his music, they seem to arise without strain, as if eternally available. This is another reason why they sound like revelations of an interior state rather than something achieved by moving out of oneself (as they might sound in Beethoven). And as we have heard, these passages are often both richly emotional and archly ultramundane, somehow both personal and

Example 2.27 Symphony 41 in C Major, K. 551, ii, bars 1–11

Example 2.27 *(Cont.)*

Example 2.27 (*Cont.*)

Example 2.28 Symphony 41 in C Major, K. 551, ii, bars 28–39

Example 2.28 (*Cont.*)

Example 2.28 (*Cont.*)

Example 2.28 *(Cont.)*

otherworldly. As such they seem to emanate from an interiorized sense of self, but one that also functions as a locus of transcendence. (Think again of the sudden onset of all those flats in the B-flat major excerpt from the Andante of K. 550 (example 2.25): the richly scored E-flat minor-seventh sonority comes on like divine afflatus—or like the seething release of latent emotion.) With this uncanny melding of the deeply personal and the transcendently suprapersonal, the inner-worldly and otherworldly, we are verging on the realm of what some have called post-Kantian subjectivity.

The occluded core of this modern construction of subjectivity is the noumenon, the opposite number of the phenomenon in Kant's transcendental analytic, the supersensible thing-in-itself, forever unavailable to human cognition. For Gary Tomlinson, "the advent of the noumenon . . . signals the fixing of a modern relation between the subject and the supersensible. Unperceived realms . . . now have been introjected into the forms of subjective knowledge."[45] Karol Berger has noted the connection between "the Kantian noumenal realm of the thing-in-itself, a realm utterly unknowable" and E.T.A. Hoffmann's "infinite realm of the spirits."[46] Implicit in Hoffmann (and later explicit in Schopenhauer) is the idea that music, like no other medium, "gives voice to this noumenal realm."[47] Music was also heard at this time to give voice to an increasingly interiorized sense of self. As Hegel put it, for example, "The proper task of music is to vivify some content or other in the sphere of subjective inner life."[48] In a pioneering probe of Mozart's music and Romantic consciousness, Marshall Brown speaks of Mozart's "revolutionary self-absorption," manifested in passages such as the slow introduction to the "Dissonance" Quartet, in which the music seems to access some preconscious realm, some deeply interior space.[49]

We have been listening for evocations of the supernatural, instances of preternatural dissonance, otherworldly purple patches—all these rapturous moments sound as oblique refractions from some other dimension, intimate an altered, heightened consciousness.[50] Mozart's music stages suspended moments of revelatory beauty, moments whose second sight is made possible by the presence of a threshold that can never be crossed, the threshold created by modern subjectivity. With this threshold, consciousness becomes an inner space created in contradistinction to the outside world, defining the outside world: to be inside is to know of an outside. Mozart's beautiful moments make this space resonate as an interior realm, activating its divination of a now remote transcendence. This unknowable otherness can only be intimated—with a brush of awe, a prickling of the senses. One is transfixed but never overmastered, fleetingly touched but never fully possessed.

Lost and Found

To gain divinatory access to this interior realm is to lose an older, easier relationship with the world: to live with the noumenon is to unlearn the everyday sense of knowing the phenomenal language of the world. Losing faith in the ability to connect with, to harmonize with, to *know* external reality, modern subjectivity moves inward, gaining an interior realm. The world is then reconceived in terms of the self, and the self begins to peer out at reality as if looking out a window. (This type of relation to reality constitutes the subjective warrant of much Romantic art, literature, and music, and is nowhere so directly conjured as in paintings such as Caspar David Friedrich's 1822 *Woman at the Window*. This painting unites two favorite themes of Friedrich and other artists of his era: the use of an open window as a threshold between inside and outside, and the presence of a *Rückenfigur*, a figure whose back is turned to the observer, thus encouraging the outward gaze, as though to gather and direct the subjective impulse out into the world beyond. In these works, the burgeoning sense of interiorized Romantic subjectivity is coupled with the scene of the bourgeois interior—the sense of being in the room is as much a part of the experience as the removed sense of space outside.[51]) In Mozart's music we can hear intimations of this new, interiorized self, still deeply suffused with a sense of what has been lost, namely, the transparent and innocent harmony of Enlightenment faith (a harmony encapsulated in Alexander Pope's freeze-dried assertion: Whatever is, is right).[52] But to lose that innocence is to find a new kind of beauty, the melancholy beauty of ironic intimation, the sound of the unreachable noumenon.

This crystallization of the relation between beauty and the loss of innocence, lingering in the aura of so much of Mozart's later instrumental music, becomes explicit in *Così fan tutte*.[53] There the main characters are disabused of their idealized view of love and fidelity to the accompaniment of astonishingly beautiful music; and the audience witnessing the ignoble deceit practiced upon the women by their male lovers also observes the demise of the cherished equation of truth and beauty, for, as Mary Hunter argues, numbers featuring remarkable musical beauty serve to frame the plot's central deceit.[54] And something closely related to this same crystallization informs the many sotto voce "sorpresa" scenes in Mozart's other operas, where after some shocking discovery the action freezes in a moment of surpassing musical beauty, marking the loss of certainty by making audible the awe of transformed consciousness.[55]

Moments granting sonic presence to such a precarious transformation cannot last, but they can be renewed. For Mozart's music is music to be reheard: the listening experience lives and lives again to anticipate and

then savor such moments.[56] The beautiful intimations we have been listening for in Mozart's music are ever renewable. As such, they offer a
model of musical experience in the modern age, for the cultural practice
of rehearing music continues to be sustained on the wager that what
music offers us is ever renewable. We stage Western art music the way
Mozart stages *his* special moments. This is because music remains our
noumenon, the *Ding an sich* we are always in the business of approaching. We routinely try to ground Western art music in other discourse sys-
tems, because we still tend to think of this music as a profound, even
oracular, utterance from a wordless transcendental realm, as something
that needs to be grounded even while we reassure ourselves that it can
never be. (For once music is grounded, the lights will come on in the
magic theater, and the show will be over.) Mozart more than anyone
taught us to rehear music as if unveiling the Grail.

And the spell has not yet been broken. For even on the postmodern
frontier, where the once infinite depths of the modern self have been compressed and flattened into an infinitely crowded surface, where the magic
theater stands empty, a *Kinderspiel* from the childhood of modernity—
even in *this* landscape, it is hard to imagine reaching a standpoint from
which Mozart's music would not register as beautiful. Despite the har-
rowing destruction of so many cherished fantasies—from Mozart's age
to our own, from the Terror of 1793 to the various terrors of the long
twentieth century—it seems we can still find ourselves exquisitely suspended in the sound of Mozart, still find ourselves haunted by his uncanny intimations. What Mozart offers to modernity is the sound of the
loss of innocence, the ever renewable loss of innocence. That such a
sound is beautiful may have nothing to do with Mozart and everything
to do with us.

III

GRACE AND RENEWAL

Thematic Returns

If man is the melancholy animal that knows he must die, so too is he the hopeful animal that knows renewal. As a basic rhythm of life, renewal is available with every onset of spring, every sunrise, every breath. In much Western art music, the potential for renewal is composed into the musical experience: an intramural renewal is enacted every time a recognizable tune returns within a movement. In the Viennese Classical style, these returns take place at many different levels, including the second four-bar phrase of a parallel period, the repeats of larger thematic groupings in sectionalized forms, the multiple thematic returns of rondo form, the singular thematic return of sonata form. Mozart has special ways of staging these last, and broadest, kinds of renewal, namely those moments in large-scale forms in which thematic material from the opening returns.

The Andante from the Piano Concerto in G Major, K. 453, offers an enchanting entrance into this aspect of Mozart's art. Its opening five-bar utterance returns four times in the course of the movement. Each of these returns is prepared differently, and each leads to a different place. The utterance itself possesses a kind of self-contained simplicity that allows it to act as a miraculous foil to all the musics that surround it. It can be heard to hold the brimming harvest of an epilogue as well as to project the lean expectancy of a prologue. Its functional presence is hard to pin down: it has been hailed as a frame, a motto, an incomplete question, an inscription, a proposition.[1]

The beginning of this utterance is almost conspicuously unassuming. And yet a kind of tension accrues, perhaps from the simplicity itself. The melody gently worries the fifth scale degree, which itself introduces a subtle instability when on top of the sonority, inviting some sort of action. When we return to the G in the second bar, it is differently colored—now

Example 3.1 Piano Concerto 17 in G Major, K. 453, ii, bars 1–8

it is the root of a first-inversion chord, resolving a dissonance (A over B). When the bass continues to descend to A, the G itself is nudged into the realm of dissonance. With its move to F-sharp (rather than F-natural), we are made to understand that the upper voice will be baulked in any attempt to descend to tonic from that fifth scale degree. Instead, a leap is generated that, in the context of the discourse up to now, is huge and hugely expressive. This surge of expressive energy completes the shift of the center of gravity from tonic to dominant, and it is followed by a big dissonance in the fourth bar and then the pregnant pause on the dominant. The gently expectant tension of the opening sonority is now matched by the expectant stasis of the final sonority, resting point of a half cadence.

Mozart's opening utterance thus enacts an everyday tonal process, in which a tonic falls to its dominant. One could even speak generically of a kind of written-out half cadence. After all, the phrase performs a very common contrapuntal approach to a cadence (5–6 over C, 7–6 over B,

Example 3.1 (*Cont.*)

7–#6 over A, 8 over G) in G. But the rhythmic life of the phrase—three bars of steady pulsing eighths that prolong each successive harmony and then cease with the dissonance of bar 4, which drains off melodically over two bars of a now stilled G-major triad—as well as the expressive crisis that arises in the middle of the phrase and then subsides: these things make the phrase into a contained dramatic utterance, a framed mini-drama, a portable set piece, one that opens and closes a motion, and then stops. As a movable harmonic transaction that emphasizes the dominant, the phrase seems constructed to be followed, to provide a fresh start into things, a portal to further doings. Once only will this phrase be followed and completed by a complementary phrase with the tonic cadence called for by the convention of periodic structure: at the very end of the movement.

The half cadence in bar 5 is followed by the expected key of C major, but as Charles Rosen observes, the expansive texture and expressive oboe melody of this section do not sound directly related to the opening

Example 3.2 Piano Concerto 17 in G Major, K. 453, ii, bars 25–38

utterance.[2] This has the effect of isolating the opening, even in its initial act of connecting to the rest of the movement. The first entrance of the piano soloist brings with it the first return of the opening phrase, which occurs after some plangent minor-mode inflections over a tonic pedal (example 3.2, bars 25–29).

After this richly hued minor-mode music, the opening utterance is a tranquil pool of clear water. Thus this phrase takes on a special presence, as a renewable refrain, which—like water—can refresh the landscape.

The first surprising tonal response to the refrain now occurs (bar 35), with a plunge into G minor, transforming the G-major half cadence from dominant to minor tonic. This kind of move has been described by Robert Winter as one of the options of the "bifocal close," in which a half cadence on the dominant may be followed either by the dominant as key area (as in many Classical-era sonata-form expositions) or by the tonic as key area (as in many recapitulations within those forms).[3] But

Example 3.2 *(Cont.)*

Example 3.2 *(Cont.)*

the reference to that convention is made more complex with the simultaneous onset of the minor mode. This promotes the arresting effect of freezing the G-major sonority into something else, in a kind of Ovidian metamorphosis.

When the refrain returns next (bar 64), it does so in G major, after a big cadence heralded by rising figures that climb out of a transposition of the darkly inflected pedal point we heard before (bars 54–63). So far we have heard the refrain in strings, then in piano: now the wind instruments perform it, bringing it to the requisite half cadence, now on a D-major sonority. And again the dominant is transformed to minor, as the piano introduces a new theme in D minor.[4]

Thus the movement has traveled tonally from C major to G minor to G major to D minor. The tonal momentum generated by this series of keys related by rising fifth continues with concentrated determination in the following developmental section, realizing a sequence whose every

Example 3.2 *(Cont.)*

station seems to move farther from the possibility of retreat: D minor leads to A minor, which leads on to E minor, then B minor, F-sharp minor, and finally C-sharp minor, with a decisively achieved pedal point on the V of C-sharp minor, a G-sharp-major sonority. With this we have reached the "point of furthest remove," to use the terminology of Leonard Ratner.[5] Though it arguably took all 86 bars of the movement so far to get to this remote place, Mozart will need only four bars to get back to his C-major refrain (example 3.3). Eschewing the logic of harmonic motion, Mozart thinks laterally, simply replacing the pitches of the V of C-sharp minor with those of the V of C major, one at a time, but doing so in a way that generates an astonishing series of chromatic harmonies. G-sharp major shifts to G-sharp minor (B for B-sharp); then E[7] (D for D-sharp); then G[7] (G for G-sharp).[6] This procedure is saved from seeming merely clever by the way Mozart stages his harmonies: expanding dynamics and register create the dawning excitement of a genial train of

Example 3.3 Piano Concerto 17 in G Major, K. 453, ii, bars 86–98

Example 3.3 (*Cont.*)

thought getting closer and closer to its goal. Perhaps the finest touch of all is the syncopated rhythm of the violins, who play as if drawn off the beat by the strong magnetic force of C major.[7]

The achieved result of these extraordinary bars is nothing other than Mozart's unassuming refrain. Here it is again, as ever, as though the world knew nothing of C-sharp minor. And yet, does not its unaltered transparency allow us to take the sharpest measure yet of C-sharp minor and all things else in the movement so far? It is here that we recognize the extent to which the opening phrase, as a renewable refrain, stands both inside and outside the plane of the movement. It offers the reflective properties of a placidly neutral surface (like the even gaze of a nonjudgmental face), as well as the ability to absorb the life of the movement. For one thing, its steady eighth-note pulse has in fact been pervasive throughout the movement: we just heard it in the bass line of the retransition,

Example 3.3 (*Cont.*)

before that in the bass line of the modulating, developmental sequence that led to C-sharp minor, and before that in the minor-mode pedal points that preceded significant cadences in C and G. In this way, the opening figure is like an emblematic motto for the rest of the movement, revealing the heart of its rhythmic life.

There are more tonal surprises ahead. The half cadence of this central refrain is followed by a warm surge of E-flat major (bar 95). This is a Schubertian modulation (as in his String Quintet in C Major, first movement—the way into the cello duet); not only does it enact a plunge into the flat side of C (which in itself seems to balance the sharp-side extremity reached before the return to C, while also achieving an intimation of interiority), but it lends the pitch G a special new color. Within the refrain, G has been colored in four different ways: an expectant fifth becomes the root of a first-inversion triad, then a dissonance over the bass, and finally a tonicized root. The music after the first appearance of the refrain transforms this rooted G back into the fifth of C; the music after the second appearance maintains the rooted

Example 3.3 *(Cont.)*

G but changes the mode. Here in bar 95 the G becomes the third of a triad, completing the color wheel with what feels like the most ingratiating transformation yet.

Contributing to the gratifying effect of this E-flat-major music are the reiterated eighth-note chords in the left hand, which directly continue the chordal treatment of the refrain. Repeated eighth-note harmonies rarely sound with such innate dignity—the Andante seems to draw itself up here, to the full height of its humanity. Elaine Sisman hears a sarabande rhythm in the refrain, and notes the continuation of this rhythm in the E-flat music—this topical identification contributes to the dignified sense of this passage.[8] To my ear, these bars offer the richest concentration of experience available within the Andante: they ring as if finding the resonance of the movement's tonal shape, while also fixing the nature of the refrain both as separable portal that can lead to any number of places and as the centering heartbeat of the movement.

The refrain itself thus carries an extraordinary, paradoxical effect of stasis and tension, of quiet self-possession and unsettling departure point.[9] Its spare features—the calm rhythmic pulsing, the shifting color of its melodic G, the ritual harmonic transaction of tonic falling to dominant: a rhythm, a central pitch, a harmonic move—may be laid out on the table like magical tokens of presence. The beauty of their collectivity is renewed over and over, as touchstone and as impetus. A sense of renewable grace suffuses these return appearances, as they both collect and release the music around them, as they emblematize, reflect, and intimate.

The Andante issues into a cadenza, after which the refrain returns for a final time, in the wind instruments (example 3.4). Sliding minor-mode inflections from elsewhere in the movement now invade the refrain, the firmness of its harmonies dissolving into running colors, bleeding right through the half cadence and on into the subdominant and a commensurate consequent phrase, undertaken by the piano and leading to a full cadence. With the advent of this completing phrase, rounding the opening phrase into a full eight-bar period, the refrain is domesticated, made to flow into the time of the piece from its vantage outside that time, made to subside into the movement, as though disappearing from view.[10]

Example 3.4 Piano Concerto 17 in G Major, K. 453, ii, 123–35

Example 3.4 (*Cont.*)

The Andante from Mozart's G-major Piano Concerto stages multiple returns of its opening material, granting that material an enchanted, talismanic presence. What happens when the urge to return is consolidated into a single recapitulation, as in sonata form? The returning first theme triggers a welcome flush of recognition, not just because it is familiar but because it is fresh all over again: its freshness is restored precisely in the way it gathers and reflects the music that has ensued, the way it sounds now as consequence as well as cause. This is a profound effect little remarked upon—usually the talk is of large-scale resolution rather than of renewal (in such accounts, return is more a structural than a psychological effect).[11] The returning theme provides the psychological experience of temporal transformation within general stability of character, which is close to the experience of selfhood. It is thus no surprise that recapitulation remains one of the hardiest impulses of Western music in the modern age. Artful returns characterize the Viennese Classical style, providing both one of its greatest charms and one of its principal dramatic rhythms. You might say that return never had it so good as in the Classical style—it is one of the special arts of the style to profile return.

The prosaically named "retransition," as the passage immediately preceding the large-scale return in sonata form, makes for a useful point of focus. The retransition can foster great drama as the reentry into the mainstream time of the piece: one thinks of many examples in Beethoven, of first themes set up to be loudly recapitulated, seeming to storm the stage, or of the quietly "impending" effect in the first movement of the *Eroica* Symphony. The retransition becomes a spot for narration, or for "styling": the theme may return as a punch line (think of a Haydn rondo finale), a dramatic apotheosis, a hallowed visitation; we may see it coming a mile off, or stumble over it of a sudden; we may be mysteriously transported there, or be on anxious alert, waiting for the other shoe to drop. Mozart had a special genius for retransition, one that reveals a distinctive attitude toward formal convention. Often after a dramatic development section reaches a climactic pedal point, Mozart's passage of retransition floats gracefully to its destination—as though to make privilege out of custom.[12]

A stunning example of this can be heard in the retransition of the first movement of the Symphony in G Minor, K. 550. During an ominously quiet section of the development, strings and winds keep alternating the sighing half-step motive from the movement's outset, until they find themselves whispering the dominant of G minor—the home dominant— to each other. Suddenly the pent-up emotion erupts (bar 153), and the basses sound the "home sigh" E-flat to D again and again, as though obsessed with some primal woe, while the rest of the orchestra writhes above like a keening congregation. Just as suddenly, the basses and all other strings are gone. With this heaving engine shut off, the winds glide gently to earth. They perform the composite rhythm of the previous bars but now as a quiet chromatic descent over a sustained dominant pedal. As the wind lines touch down, they overlap exquisitely with the opening version of the sighing motive, which then continues on as the returning first theme. The presence of this overlap allows the winds their effect of making a perfect landing, not just onto the outset of the first theme but onto its first strongly felt downbeat.

The most fundamental return of the movement, its largest preordained rhythm, is thus brought about as though without effort. Or as though

Example 3.5 Symphony 40 in G Minor, K. 550, i, bars 153–68

Example 3.5 (Cont.)

Example 3.5 *(Cont.)*

one cannot arrive by trying, but by letting go. The opening theme does not return as the duty of appointed convention but rather *reappears* in an absorbing new context. This renewal entails a deft psychological shift: the E-flat–D motive that sobbed so obsessively at the end of the development is now re-experienced as a gently persistent appoggiatura, like a latent trauma repressed back into a symptom. But this is a symptom that we now know contains a world of trauma—not for nothing do some hear this recapitulation as tragic acquiescence to utter despair.[13]

Here and elsewhere, arrival on the home dominant creates a direct tonal link to the return of the main theme. It is also very common for major-mode Classical-style retransitions to commence with a pedal point on the V of vi. As Rosen and others have explained, the submediant key area serves as the "point of furthest remove" in many middle sections, a

Example 3.5 (*Cont.*)

tonal habit from the Baroque. It thus acts as a kind of continental divide, signaling that things will now begin to move back toward the conditions of the outset. The convention was often condensed: composers began to arrive at the dominant of the submediant, avoiding the cadence on the submediant and moving instead back to the movement's tonic. This creates a space between the V of vi and the ensuing tonic, a space with interesting possibilities.[14]

Sometimes Mozart simply jumps over the space, allowing the gap to create a small shock when we suddenly hear the main theme back in the initial key area. Not only is the cadence on the submediant evaded, but the main key returns without preamble. In the Finale of the Piano Sonata in F Major, K. 280, Mozart ratchets up the comedy of this tonal shock with a bracing registral disjunction.

Example 3.6 Piano Sonata in F Major, K. 280, iii, bars 102–11

Roman Ivanovitch cites a more poetic version of this leap from V of vi directly to tonic. In the C-Major Andante of Mozart's last string quartet (K. 590), four bars of E major as V of A minor lead to a trilled turn figure on E in the now solo first violin.[15] This exposed figure could easily cadence in A minor. Instead, the E is treated retroactively as the third of C major, and the first theme returns with the rest of the quartet texture. (This kind of move, a common-tone modulation emphasizing root motion of a third, would become a staple of tonal magic in the generation to come.)

In terms of harmonic function, progression by fifths would seem the most prosaic way to bridge this space: V of vi moves to VI, then II, then V, then I (with each of these functions usually represented by a nondiatonic seventh chord). Versions of this progression can be found in each of Mozart's last three symphonies, and they are anything but prosaic. The development section of the E-flat-major Andante from Mozart's G-minor Symphony, K. 550, slowly hikes its bass line up in half steps, from B-flat to G, the V of vi. After a prolongation of that sonority which itself includes a remarkably condensed sequence of fifths (bar 67), a four-bar sequence leads back to the opening key and theme through the circle of fifths: G^7 to C^7 to F^7 to B-flat^7 (example 3.7). This harmonic sequence is beautifully embellished with wind figures that derive from the striking bass line way back in bar 2, now combined with the chirruping thirty-second notes so populous throughout the movement.

The Andante cantabile of the "Jupiter" Symphony, K. 551, also features an embellished path through the circle of fifths (example 3.8). In this case, Mozart arrives on the V of vi (A major; the key of the movement is F) and confirms it three times over two bars, realizing a slow hemiola rhythm. He then backs up a fifth harmonically, to E^7, and launches a string of fifths that leads to the returning tonic and first theme: E^7, A^7, D^7, G^7, C^7, F. Leisurely sextuplets decorate the dissonant upper structure of each harmony, creating elaborate turn figures around each chord seventh that include a fleeting ninth at the top of the swirl.

The first movement of Mozart's Symphony in E-flat Major, K. 543, provides a minimalist version of the same progression (example 3.9). A

Example 3.7 Symphony 40 in G Minor, K. 550, ii, bars 69–75

Example 3.7 (*Cont.*)

loud driving passage heading to a cadence in C minor (vi in E-flat) is dramatically interrupted after its dominant (G, or V/vi) by a bar of silence. Then the winds alone offer three quiet sonorities—C⁷, F⁷, and B-flat⁷—connected with chromatic voice leading and each decorated with a single minor-ninth appoggiatura, perhaps the most concisely potent expressive embellishment imaginable.[16]

Time can seem to stand still in passages like these, which creates an audible paradox, for it is just at this moment that the large-scale time of the movement is being marked most emphatically (namely, by the onset of the return of the main theme and main key). Most remarkable of all is that Mozart needs no exotic musical language to pull this off—the falling-fifth sequence is no rarified figure of speech but rather a banal and clichéd harmonic progression. Rosen observes that the falling-fifth sequence, while often deployed as a driving force in Baroque music, has the effect of treading water in the Classical style.[17] Mozart uses it for just this

Example 3.7 (*Cont.*)

effect in many of his retransitions—it brings about a feeling of floating gently and effortlessly down to the appointed resolution. This type of harmonic sequence performs work without seeming to work: the local passing of one dominant relation to another, the often beautifully wrought textures that Mozart puts into play at just these moments, all conspire to take us off the tracks of time, precisely at musical time's biggest juncture.[18] Or, better, the sequence has the effect of divorcing time's progress from human effort—it seems to run by itself, apart from, and regardless of, our interventions. The effect is of otherworldly calm, as though to quiet the noise of local time, so that we can hear the passing of global time.

The Adagio movement of the String Quintet in D Major, K. 593, enhances this effect of otherworldly calm by means of an extreme disjunction. In a developmental elaboration leading up to the recapitulated first theme, dotted rhythms from the opening theme gather into a strangely disorienting imitative passage, beginning in bar 44 and culminating in a

Example 3.8 Symphony 41 in C Major, K. 551, ii, bars 55–60

Example 3.9 Symphony 39 in E-flat Major, K. 543, i, bars 177–88

great stretto, which sets up tremendous cadential pressure to resolve to the submediant of the home tonic. What happens next is even more extraordinary. Charles Rosen's description would be hard to surpass:

> The climax is the sudden creation of a void: a cadence, built up powerfully and with the fierce energy that the cumulated descent can arouse, is, in measure 52, *not* played—not only postponed but permanently withheld. Instead of the cadence, all motion ceases, and with a sudden *piano* only the soft throbbing of the two violas is left. As the other instruments enter with a new sequence that leads directly back to the main theme, we find four completely different kinds of rhythm superimposed in a contrapuntal texture at once complex and deeply touching. . . . The sequence and the superimposition of rhythmic textures achieve a condition of stillness after the vigorous descent [of thirds]: everything is resolved quietly and

Example 3.10 String Quintet in D Major, K. 593, ii, bars 44–60

Example 3.10 (*Cont.*)

inevitably, suspended motionless almost without breath after the arrest of impulse by the daring non-cadence.

To Rosen's account I would only add that the gestures of first violin and cello (starting at the upbeat to bar 54) behave as if displaced from the gravitational action of the contrapuntal braid in the violas, and that this displacement does more than anything else to sustain the otherworldly air of this passage. Those ranging pizzicato leaps in the cello are unlike anything heard so far in the movement and possess an other-dimensional, runic quality of voice. And the calm preternaturally *rising* steps of the first violin speak of Olympian indifference, as though disengaged from the downward tide of the sequence. And yet each part does indeed relate

Example 3.10 (*Cont.*)

to the prevailing harmonic action: the first violin executes a voice exchange with the dotted-rhythm line in the second violin, thus ghosting along with the sequence; and the cello enunciates the roots of a falling fifth progression that moves completely round the circle, from G^7 back to G as tonic, as if traversing the harmonic world from a supramundane standpoint. The cello and first violin comport with each other like jaded gods playing cards behind the scenes; we encounter them in some timeless realm, or a realm that is all time.[19]

Mozart knows another kind of magic for moving from V/vi to home dominant, one that is more a matter of harmonic transformation. Instead of moving by steps of a fifth, he deploys lateral thinking, in which voice leading acts as an alchemical agent.[20] One of the best-known examples of this kind of transformation occurs in the retransition of the first movement of the Piano Sonata in F Major, K. 332. The stage is set by arriving onto A (V/vi) with an augmented sixth resolution. Three different harmonies appear, each the result of a minimal note change: A major shifts to A minor; A minor shifts to C^7 in second inversion.

Example 3.11 Piano Sonata in F Major, K. 332, i, bars 122–36

The murmuring E and F alternation in the right hand changes hue with each shift, until the last harmony regroups into root position and a higher register (bar 131), as though to introduce the returning theme with a bit more ceremony. Wye Jamison Allanbrook captures the playful logic of this transition with her analogy of "word golf," a game in which one word morphs into another, a letter at a time (and with each intervening stage forming yet another word, as in cat-cot-dot-dog).[21]

Perhaps the most magical retransition in all of Mozart occurs in the finale of the "Jupiter" Symphony, where he follows a heightened version of the V/vi convention with a passage of matchless inspiration. It is worth capturing some of the preceding context, in order to sharpen our sense of this marvelous effect. The development section of this sublimely learned finale is almost exclusively concerned with a kind of filler theme from what topical analysts might call the "verve" section of the exposition, in which a dotted-rhythm head motive rolls down a scale, bumping lightly on each degree of the triad.[22] After an early arrival on the V of vi (nine bars into the development and sustained for seven bars), these scale figures are deployed with stretto-like bursts that move regularly downward through the circle of fifths: through A minor, then D minor, then G, then C. When F arrives (bar 185), the process goes into reverse: now most of the scales ascend, and the keys progress by upward fifth: F to C minor to G minor to D minor to A minor. The movement's motto-like opening motive appears after each stage and effects the modulation up a fifth. After reaching D minor (bar 201), an extended version of the opening motive moves the tonal action through A minor all the way to the dominant of E minor (V/iii in the home key of C). This is the "point of furthest remove," one degree more distant than the usual V/vi and as far as one can possibly go in this line (the logical next step, V/vii, does not exist in the major mode). A retransition-style pedal point ensues at bar 209, using both descending and ascending forms of the rolling scale.

So the entire development has moved back and forth by fifths (A minor, D minor, G major, C major, F major, C minor, G minor, D minor, A minor, E minor) and now finds itself churning away on this final station, miles away from home. What next? Suddenly everything relaxes; all that's left is the dotted-rhythm motive in the bassoons (bar 219). The linear move from B major (as V of E minor) back to the V of C is as astonishing as it is simple in concept: the D-sharp–F-sharp dyad stays put, while the bass slides downward below it by half step (from B to B-flat, A, A-flat, G) and a C is added in a middle voice. From this lateral movement in the bass a series of beautiful hues emerges effortlessly, as well as the more directed sound of a harmony being assembled tone by tone, namely the augmented-sixth chord with both A-flat and F-sharp, looking to resolve onto the home dominant. Many other composers, having struck upon this wonderful expedient, may have been tempted to cap the train of thought with a "rescue" six-four, letting the D-sharp–F-sharp resolve upward to E–G. Instead Mozart pushes the dyad down to D–F, creating a full dominant seventh, and adding a suspended C on top. This preserves the overall sinking aspect of the passage, while also making the C on the downbeat a bit more dissonant: in the six-four version it would dissonate against the bass alone; as part of a V^7 it dissonates against the D as well as the bass. The C also supports the dissonant F with an overtone-like fifth, giving the chord seventh more bite.

Example 3.12 Symphony 41 in C Major, K. 551, iv, bars 209–28

Example 3.12 (*Cont.*)

In addition to being such a special tone in terms of dissonance treatment, the C in the first violins launches one more downward rolling scale: and this one rolls right into the return of the main theme. Thus the theme drops into place, as though without effort. The entire transition is a miracle of buoyant concentration: its four linear half steps seem to take back the entire development, to absorb and transcend all that sublime contrapuntal commotion so busily mapping out the world, fifth by fifth by fifth.

In these examples and many others Mozart drives to a dramatic climax, and then, as if turning off the engines, glides down to the return of his primary theme. Why? Why should time seem to stop *here*—at the very moment we are about to experience the most inevitable, most explicit,

Example 3.12 (*Cont.*)

least disguised formal junction of the movement? Why is this the place that leaves human agency behind, with a bejeweled, mechanically automatic sequence, or with some breathtaking voice leading that sidesteps syntax and opens magic doors into other dimensions?

Mozart's graceful landings transform thematic renewal into an act of grace. Here Schiller's *Anmut*, grace as beauty in motion, rises to a higher orbit and becomes *Gnade*, the dispensation of grace. Here at the most consequential fulcrum of the entire form, the heavy structural downbeat lands light as a feather; the inevitable becomes the miraculous. Return is staged not as an act of resolution, not as a thing willed—but as a thing granted. Form as *Gnade*, then, as gift: the great thematic redoubling of sonata form is performed not as an enactment of convention but as a miracle of renewal.

Example 3.12 *(Cont.)*

The Open Close

The conventional return of an opening theme seems a natural place to experience renewal and even—in a Mozartean world—grace. But can a similar sense of grace and renewal lighten the most inevitable convention of all, the very close of a movement or a multimovement composition? Wye Allanbrook has argued that closure in "Classic music" is almost always of a comic cast, even in contexts where one might feel justified to expect something heavier. One such context is the end of the opera *Don Giovanni*.

"This is how it ends for evildoers: They die the way they live" ("Questo è il fin di chi fa mal, e de' perfidi la morte alla vita è sempre ugual"): thus the concluding moral of *Don Giovanni*, sung by Giovanni's rattled but

relieved victims in the aftermath of his supernatural exit. The right to
such major-mode moralizing was disputed at times during the reception
of this opera, and many nineteenth-century productions did without the
epilogue, closing instead with the jarring spectacle of Giovanni's destruction. This kind of production is anachronistically depicted in the film
Amadeus, where the opera's abrupt ending leaves us slack-jawed, like
ocean voyagers discovering too late that the earth is indeed flat. But the
world is round after all, and the *mores* of the eighteenth century must
close around the wound, the gaping hole in the social fabric. As Allanbrook puts it:

> The *lieto fine* ("happy ending") was of course habitual in the late
> eighteenth century; somehow, no matter what the depredations,
> proper orders were reestablished and their restoration celebrated.
> This celebration ought not to be considered the result of "mere
> convention"; it emanates from a distinct point of view which, es-
> chewing satirical or tragical exaggerations of the way the world is,
> chooses to assert instead the goods of continuity and order, and the
> equilibrium of good sense.[23]

Part of the equilibrium achieved by Mozart in his epilogue has to do
with the way that frightening aspects of what just happened are woven
into the celebration. In the G-major tableau, Donna Anna sings the words
"Ah certo è l'ombra che l'incontrò" with an ombra-style chromatic descent over a pedal point (bars 700–706). Within the concluding D-major
Presto, scale figures return, but now they energize the sustained notes of
"E de' perfidi" with a two-octave surge that grows in volume as it ascends
(bars 788–93). "Morte" reigns again, now as an exaggerated agogic accent
that occurs twice (bars 794–98 and 819–23), its harmonic sting dulled
to a flat seventh over the tonic, nodding to the subdominant. Later (bars
837–42), the word "sempre" is set with yet another chromatic descent
over a pedal. And here the ombra is finally dissipated, draining away over
the last prolonged dominant of the opera—for everything is now drawn
into D major, the opera's ultimate center of gravity, which radiates light
and absorbs darkness. Even the curtain-closing music offers a last, delicate
depiction of Giovanni's fall, the once starkly horrifying descent woven
into a sequence that spins lightly home, as though all the fierce trappings
of death and damnation were here summoned back into a box of stage
properties, the genie slipping back into the bottle (example 3.13).[24]
Critics under the sway of powerful end-oriented works by Beethoven
came to regret Mozart's lighter manner at the conclusion of some of his
darkest minor-mode instrumental compositions. One of these, the Piano
Concerto in D Minor, K. 466, closes with a tune that Allanbrook classes

Example 3.13 *Don Giovanni*, Act 2, Finale, bars 861–71

Example 3.13 (*Cont.*)

with other Mozartean closing tunes "so unmistakably joyous in their comic spontaneity that they cannot fail to persuade us—if only momentarily—of the validity of the comic close."[25]

To create a context for Allanbrook's tune, it is worth taking in everything that happens after the final cadenza (example 3.14). The melodramatic solo theme takes the stage again, as one would expect. From this point on, it should sound once through and then lead into some cadential noise in D minor. Instead, the theme gets one phrase off and then steps on the wrong diminished-seventh chord, explodes, and is never heard from again. What settles into the space suddenly left open is a recast version of the closing theme from the finale's exposition, now in D major and

Example 3.13 (*Cont.*)

Fine dell' Opera

unfolding comfortably over a dominant pedal point. This is a reassuring sound; much like the final scene of Giovanni, the status quo returns, the storm is over.

But Mozart is not done yet. After some rousing D-major music (bars 383–88) featuring the same frenzied repeating eighth-note string texture that stirred the pot so dramatically earlier in the movement (as in bars 31–57), a further modified version of the closing theme emerges: Allanbrook's "unmistakably joyous" tune (example 3.15). Here the closing theme is broken into four short-breathed utterances, while its harmony yo-yos back to tonic every other bar. The first two bars retain the outset of the closing-theme tune, the next two throw an excited shout up to the

Example 3.14 Piano Concerto 20 in D Minor, K. 466, iii, bars 346–63

Example 3.15 Piano Concerto 20 in D Minor, K. 466, iii, bars 395–402

major third; the first two bars return, the final two answer with a toy soldier's triadic call in trumpet and horn.

By activating the mechanical joys of the toy box, this tune seals the mood—with sounds like these, there can be no returning to the troubled minor mode. After the repetition of Allanbrook's tune, the triadic call floods the texture, and we seem to find ourselves inside some whirring calliope, or musical clock (example 3.16): the two-bar toy figure in the brass triggers the same figure in the winds, and these together form a four-bar unit that is out of phase with a four-bar unit in the piano and strings, in which a rising scale in tenths, like the release of a windup spring, triggers a mechanical cadence in the strings. The invigorating mechanism continues, with stretto imitations of the toy triad sounding amid sewing-machine figuration in the strings, all over a tonic pedal with flat-seven emphasis on the subdominant. The tympani roll is the last device put into play, tripping the final cadential switch. The orchestra falls silent.

What are we hearing here? *Babes in Toyland*? Windup figurines marching in coordinated arrays, delivering smart salutes to enchanted children? And whatever happened to the dangerous energy of the finale's opening theme, always ready to leap onto an electric diminished-seventh chord, not to mention the portentous stirrings of the first movement, or the shocking metastasis of minor mode exposed at the very heart of the otherwise placidly beautiful Romanze? Are we now hearing a desperate concentration of innocence, needfully conjoined after the scorching flames of the furnace of mortality? Or shall we construe this ending as a mockery of all that drama, childish playthings overrunning the more serious doings of the rest of the concerto, Mozart laughingly degrading "finis coronat opus" into "finis deridet opus"?

Example 3.16 Piano Concerto 20 in D Minor, K. 466, iii, bars 409–28

Example 3.16 (Cont.)

Questions like these arise from a sensibility that postdates Mozart, one hungry for deeply felt extremes of experience, and for narratives that can absorb those extremes, including narratives of self-subverting irony. And, more fundamentally, one that demands the musical simulacrum of a continuous, forward-moving subjectivity, which makes such narratives necessary and plausible. But what if all the *Sturm und Drang* music in this concerto is worn as lightly as this closing music? Perhaps we are simply hearing yet another musical role—comic closure—undertaken by

Example 3.16 (*Cont.*)

a composer who can put such things on or off in an instant. And yet the pronounced childlike note in the epilogue indicates a particular styling of conventional comic closure. Its extreme contrast to the impassioned temperament of the rest of the concerto may be why it's there: drama to the point of tragic experience; comedy to the point of enchanted innocence. A balance is drawn, in terms peculiar to Mozart.

The ending to the G-minor String Quintet, K. 516, has troubled critics to a much greater extent than the ending to K. 466. Here the entire final Allegro is in the major mode, and this after three foregoing movements and a slow introduction to the finale that must be classed among the

Example 3.16 (*Cont.*)

most darkly inspired in all of Mozart. Moreover, the closing Allegro is relentlessly untroubled, almost manic in its ebullient machinations. Listen to its opening theme (example 3.17), how it whisks up to the high B. Much is being swept up and away here. Contrast this with the pensive office performed by the cello at the outset of the Adagio introduction to this movement (example 3.18) or with the fretful opening theme of the first movement (example 3.19). Soon the finale makes light work of the opening movement's pathos-ridden transitional theme (example 3.20a and b). Then the sinuous troubled chromaticism from earlier in

Example 3.17 String Quintet in G Minor, K. 516, iv, bars 1–8 of Allegro theme

Example 3.18 String Quintet in G Minor, K. 516, iv, Adagio, bars 1–2

Example 3.19 String Quintet in G Minor, K. 516, i, bars 1–4

Example 3.20a String Quintet in G Minor, K. 516, i, bars 29–39

Example 3.20a (*Cont.*)

Example 3.20b String Quintet in G Minor, K. 516, iv, bars 230–38

the opening movement is trippingly revisited, now accompanied by mock sobs in the second violin and first viola (example 3.21a and b). These parodic gestures come on as if to show us not what the comic spirit can "overcome," but what it can be equal to, namely the almost unbearable pathos of much of the rest of the quintet.

In some ways, the finale offers the unchecked spring flood of a major mode that has been making increasing inroads upon the prevailing minor-mode pathos of the composition. In the first movement, the conventional modulation to B-flat major is delayed, and a melody with the clear aspect of a second theme is presented in the lingering tonic minor (see example 3.20a). And when B-flat major finally arrives, it projects a vehemence that offers no relaxation from the prevailing restlessness of the movement. The next movement (Minuet) is again governed by G minor, but the onset of the Trio section transforms the Minuet's bleakly

Example 3.21a String Quintet in G Minor, K. 516, i, bars 20–24

Example 3.21b String Quintet in G Minor, K. 516, iv, bars 248–52

drawn cadence into a major-mode figure budding gently into life (example 3.22). This comes on like a small miracle—with a simple mode change, a dark close becomes a warming start. But like all Trios, this one is framed by its Minuet, and its uplift of loveliness remains a charmed memory. The Adagio movement takes up residence in *con sordino* E-flat major, but the mode darkens quite suddenly both in the first section and the recapitulating final section. These minor-mode interpolations serve to profile the poignant swell of emotion that follows, when the major mode returns unforgettably (see the discussion of example 2.26). Although minor-mode music is thus transcended by major-mode music within the

Example 3.22 String Quintet in G Minor, K. 516, ii, bars 37–49

bounds of this movement, the Adagio's key of E-flat major remains within the overall penumbra of G minor. As if to make this tonal hierarchy unimpeachable, a second Adagio commences, in a G minor that now seems walled in, steeping in the highest concentration yet of its pathos (example 3.23). The harmonic and melodic materials at its outset are uncomplicated: the facts of minor made plain. When the harmony begins to move afield, it is only to move along the walls of the prison, taking the full measure of its indwelling resonance. Anguished sixteenth notes in the violin begin to rain like blows upon G minor's implacable dominant (bars 30–32). But then the bass drops away, and the sixteenth notes find themselves tapping away on a suddenly lighter dominant.[26] The repeating figure drifts upward, from A to C, from C to E, still attached to the dominant but now casting a timidly hopeful glance toward G major. And then the somber descending line from the Adagio's outset is heard again in the first violin, now in major, now as a series of tentative steps, as though toward an unaccustomed light.

The rest is jouissance, edgy only in its moments of parody, but even there with a kind of racing, wind-in-the-face glee. If the Adagio introduction is all about the inescapable hold of G minor, the Allegro finale seems all about the inability of G minor to touch us ever again. The contrast could not be more extreme: one moment we are sinking ever inward, lamenting the losses that unstring the heart, one by one, until the slackness of oblivion is all that's left; the next we are impishly plying the wind, shot into flight by a tautly strung bow.

In the flow of such richly contrasting invention, Mozart's compositional persona moves like some preternatural actor, able to exchange staggeringly different roles in an instant. Allanbrook refers to his "quicksilver" shifts

Example 3.23 String Quintet in G Minor, K. 516, iv, Adagio into Allegro

Example 3.23 (Cont.)

Example 3.23 (*Cont.*)

from one topic to the next.[27] And Martin Geck is on to something similar when he summarizes Mozart's compositional freedom with the cry: "Harlequin componiert!" Whereas later composers and thinkers *reflect* on Freedom, says Geck, Mozart *composes* Freedom.[28] Thus he is Harlequin, eternally light on his feet, equal to any situation, the flash of his checkered costume like chiaroscuro in motion. And this freedom finds gratifying amplification at just those moments when the composer would seem most constrained, such as at conventional returns and endings. Mozart's music belies the connotations of terms like "finale" and "final cadence," for he almost always ends with a sense of lifting off, an acceleration of spirit.

One of the most ingratiating compositions in this regard is the Finale of the G-major Piano Concerto, K. 453. The variation movement that closes the concerto seems to personify the spirit of high comedy. Its theme

Example 3.23 (*Cont.*)

Example 3.23 (*Cont.*)

is already funny, with an eighth-note flourish after each subphrase in the A section, and again at the end of the B section (example 3.24). With repeats, we hear this comic salute six times. The regular disposition of this 32-bar theme is maintained through five variations. Mozart gradually raises the level of contrast, up to the shocking shift that occurs when the shambling shadows of the G-minor fourth variation are abruptly scattered by the stirring gusts of the G-major fifth variation. Starting in bar 160 of example 3.25, an extraordinary passage tropes the last four bars of this final variation, reenacting and extending the stepwise descent in the bass from C down to D just heard in bars 156–59. Upward chromatic lines in the piano mark each stage of the descent, and syncopated suspensions in the strings seem to tap the brakes, gently slowing the pre-

Example 3.23 (*Cont.*)

Example 3.24 Piano Concerto 17 in G Major, K. 453, iii, bars 1–16 (first violin only)

vailing momentum of the variations heard so far.[29] Finally the piano breaks out of its chain-link chromaticism with a lyrical flourish that sings the music to a full stop on the dominant, followed by a long breath of

Example 3.25 Piano Concerto 17 in G Major, K. 453, iii, bars 160–74

Example 3.26 Piano Concerto 17 in G Major, K. 453, iii, bars 330–46

silence that may or may not be filled with an improvised lead-in by the soloist.

After that breath, an extensive "finale to the finale" follows, lifting the tempo to a fleet Presto. Often compared to an opera buffa finale, this section rolls out with much garrulous redoubling of material, including toy fanfares, churning cadential whirlpools, ombra passages that steal across the stage, and hastily stacked imitative entries a fourth apart. The first half of the movement's theme appears again, now bustled through the general onrush. After the doubled cadential drive that ends in bar 330, the theme returns one last time, quietly and with pizzicato strings underneath (example 3.26). Its four-bar phrases, so absolutely regular throughout, are here extended by comic iterations of its eighth-note closing salute. Mechanically going up after the first phrase, mechanically coming down after the second, these mocking echoes seem intent on unmasking

Example 3.26 (*Cont.*)

the ridiculously simple gestural mechanism of the theme. And then the close, with its fourfold repetition of the same rhythmic motive: yet another mocking gesture, and one entrusted with the task of concluding the entire concerto. Or is all this motivic proliferation the sound of exuberant affirmation rather than mockery? Of course it is both.

Such spirited redoublings form a primary staple of Mozartean comedy. They occur in chattering local repetitions but also in the immediate repetition of entire phrases or sections (such as occur in this "finale to the finale" but also in the final scene of *Don Giovanni*). They may be sparked by what just happened, they may even start off as mockery, but they soon generate their own momentum, as if joyously foaming over. *Joie de vivre* takes over, as when Snoopy launches into that uncontrollable happy-feet dance, or when youngsters begin running all over the place, laughing and shrieking like a house on fire. Children find these moments often, sliding into them as a natural extension of their energy. It is tempting to conclude that with endings like the ones we've been listening to, Mozart turns us into children once again—or at least reminds us what the surplus energy of childhood feels like.

This sense of innocence regained, this return to a childlike outlook, is yet another form of Mozartean lightness. For to close like this is almost as if to deny the weight of experience. To feel such lightness at the conclusion of a piece of music, at the place where accumulated knowledge might have banished innocence, is to hear once again why Mozart's music continually energizes, rather than drains. But of course what we have regained is not innocence itself but rather the embrace of innocence. Mozart composes into his endings an effect not unlike the mustering of a theatrical cast at curtain call: the tragically demolished hero once again fleet on his feet, hands clasped all round, bows and smiles, the entertainment approved, ratified, in a collective embrace of illusion, of innocent fantasy, that cherished remnant of childhood. In doing so, Mozart offers us what we might call the "open close." A small curtain comes down, so that a larger curtain may rise. With the sound of the open close, the spirit lightens once again, as if only now sprung into readiness for what lies ahead. Restored to the world. Renewed.

KNOWING INNOCENCE

To conclude with the notion of renewal may seem as though to slide the capstone of a Christological narrative neatly into place. After all, we began with thoughts of perfection, of the perfect made musical, like the spirit made flesh, or the corporeal made light as spirit; we ventured into realms of human expressivity, experienced visitations of elevated consciousness in liminal moments that "unveil the Grail"; we spoke of a loss of innocence, then we spoke of grace, and now of renewal. And in the case of *Ave verum corpus*, we heard how Mozart's sacred music limns the Christian mystery of redemption by sublimating its own indwelling means of expression.

Perfection, revelation, incarnation, grace, redemption. Such metaphors resonate throughout the history of Mozart reception.[1] We probably should not be surprised at their ubiquity, the ease of their fit over the past two centuries. Mozart's seemingly infallible musical judgment, accounts of his miraculous ease, coupled with the Romantic notion of music as a mystically potent, invisible force make perceptions like these seem second nature. If Mozart's music has not maintained an explicitly Christlike presence, it has at the very least been perceived as a locus of goodness. And yet one does not experience anything like the perfected motion of Christian temporality. Mozart's music offers no master narrative of Paradise Lost and Regained, of overcoming and salvation. Rather Mozart stops just this side of damnation, and just this side of redemption.[2] A kind of innocence is always in play, but not as origin and telos. Instead I have spoken of an "ever renewable loss of innocence." To accept this notion is also to lay claim to an ever renewable embrace of innocence. Mozart teaches us that innocence can be a continually available rejuvenation of spirit rather than an all-or-nothing quality, once lost, lost forever.

In broad cultural terms, it is tempting to interpret the end of the age of Enlightenment as a loss of innocence, a loss of innocent faith in the transparency of the world. Romanticism then emerges as the opening up of a new space, both within and beyond, a space fashioned by loss but enchanted by longing.[3] Mozart meets us at the *threshold* of this space, which is more or less the burden of E.T.A. Hoffmann's assessment of Mozart in relation to Haydn and Beethoven. Transcendence and interiority are both intimated, rather than achieved. This is how I have chosen to hear those emergent passages that seem to lift off from the prevailing musical discourse, like a visitation of altered consciousness.[4] But even more generally, Mozart's music can be heard to hover: between innocence and experience, ideality and sensuousness, comedy and tragedy, sympathy and mockery, intimacy and transcendence.[5] It offers no blind faith yet no paralyzing doubt; it is not just a longingly imperfect reach for the infinite (Schiller's sentimental art) nor just a comfortably perfect grasp of the finite (Schiller's naïve art); it is childlike yet knowing.

This continuous hovering is like a perpetual onset of ironic self-consciousness, humming as an alternating current with its continual loss of, renewal of, innocence. Mozart's music seems always on the verge of full self-consciousness, but never so far as to lose its grace, the fate of that young man in Kleist's "On the Marionette Theater," who accidentally observes his graceful movements in a mirror and then can never replicate them. Mozart's music seems both to enact unselfconsciously and to be always aware of its own role playing. Within the context of the comic operas, his music seems both to sympathize with his characters and to mock them, to give them both puppet strings and souls.[6]

But the result of this ironic hovering is not some sort of neutralized stasis, despite claims for Mozart's objectivity. Remember the theologian Karl Barth's appeal to a consoling turn in Mozart's music, in which "the light rises and the shadows fall, though without disappearing, in which joy overtakes sorrow without extinguishing it."[7] Barth's image invokes a tropism, a quality and direction of motion rather than a completed motion. We can transfer his sense of "light rising and shadows falling" onto the lightness of Mozart's musical discourse, the hovering quality we have been listening for. This is music whose energy keeps it always on the rise, always buoyant. At times we are granted the pure, weightless pleasure of processes that seem to run by themselves, or that run without any sign of strain. Think again of all those bejeweled sequences, how they arise so easily, spin so effortlessly, as if to remind us of reassuringly eternal orbits. Remember so many of Mozart's retransitions, where the music glides to a big rhythmic node as if transcending human agency. Or think of the suspended apartness, the rapt sonorous envelope in the very first examples we listened to; or the out-of-phase, floating lines that generate unearthly dissonances; or the oblique key centers and tonal colorings that foster deeply expressive purple patches.

This recourse to the oblique and out-of-phase can be heard as a general sense of rhythmic freedom—the ability to let events float sidelong to each other, in ways that create that special liminal sense of an extra dimension, a dimension oblique to normative temporality. Time can come to seem suspended at such moments precisely because the passage of time is so crucial to the general perception of Mozart's style, as Karol Berger has recently argued in his book *Bach's Cycle, Mozart's Arrow*. In a music so fundamentally expressive of the forward motion of time from event to event, so pervaded by punctuation and expectation, we are always aware of where we are in the form, always anticipating the arrival of the next event.[8] Such a musical style can more effectively stage moments that seem to stop this arrow in its flight. In many of Mozart's gliding retransitions, this effect is brought on by a falling-fifth sequence—a piece of cyclical harmonic motion arising within a style that moves largely by cadential progression.[9] In all those passages I have characterized as liminal, such as "purple" expansions from the middle of the phrase, or out-of-phase dissonance, oblique rhythmic freedom loosens stricter imperatives of phrase rhythm. Even the floating textures of the Clarinet Concerto's Adagio, or "Soave sia il vento"—pulsing or undulating accompaniments with a slower-moving melody—are enabled by the oblique temporal experience of combining different rates of passage and thus attenuating any concerted sense of relentless forward motion.[10]

Another kind of freedom finds play in the deft lightness of so many of Mozart's unforced, instantaneous transformations. A fresh burst of invention is always available, like a burst of acceleration, or a burst of joy: another tune always on tap; another topic, another texture, suddenly *there*; another level of consciousness just an intake of breath away. Expressive chromaticism arises without strain in the middle of a melody; harmony instantly plunges flatward, into an always accessible interiority that never cloys.

We are ever aware of the pervasive availability of invention in Mozart's music, which creates a broad effect of pervasive renewal and rejuvenation. It is as though he transforms the ever available lightness of consciousness into music. For Mozart's music captures the mobility of consciousness, as a fluid, human medium; the gracefulness of consciousness, in its weightless maneuvering; and the grace of consciousness, as a crucial endowment of identity, the gift of self-awareness.

The ironic self-consciousness I am eager to hear in Mozart is no longer an emanation of the world or the divine, as in some primary strains of premodern Western thought. But neither has it yet been pulled into the gravitational field of modern interiority. Rather we seem suspended in a Kantian moment, in which the external world has been sundered from us, lying forever beyond reach on the other side of the scrim of

consciousness—but also in which this same consciousness is newly em-
powered to create its own reality. Moreover, Mozart's music forever bur-
bles up as if from the childhood of this latter notion, reveling in creative
invention rather than burdened with re-creating the world over and over.

Irony, as a precipitate of consciousness, comes in many concentra-
tions. The *Grundton* of Mozartean irony is not Mephistophelian negation; he is not exposing cherished human affairs as so much tawdry theater. Nor is he about to entertain the Quixotic irony of conflating the
fantastical with the everyday. There is a strong sense that Mozart's music
lives knowingly in a world of beautiful appearances, a consoling realm
for fallen spirits who have lost the key to things as they are.[11] And yet
this Fall registers as a rising buoyancy: Mozartean irony is always also a
readiness for innocence.

Like ironic consciousness, Mozart's music is a weightless suffusion
that both mimics and creates, reflects and illuminates. We might say that
Mozart's music makes ironic consciousness opaque. The beauty that results is as real as a rainbow. And thus Mozart helps us understand how
beauty can materialize as a special opacity of consciousness, as an intimate, ever available, endearment of identity: we like who we are when
we are aware of the beautiful.

But we are back where we began, weighing pronouncements about Mozart. Having propagated my share of them, I find myself standing along-
side all those who have been tempted to give voice to their enchantment
with Mozart. As I recede for good into this happy company, I wish for
Mozart to emerge once more, with a musical phrase that has accompanied me as a kind of motto through the time of these writings. I invite
you to savor its knowing innocence, how it opens both outward and inward, leaves a finger's touch on the heart, then closes with a graceful fall.

"Laudate Dominum," from *Vesperae Solennes de Confessore*, K. 339, bars 1–4

That such a phrase then continues, growing into a sweet song of praise, seems an almost unspeakable act of grace. No wonder we have chosen to greet the sound of Mozart with so many spoken acts of gratitude.

NOTES

Invitation

1. Karl Barth, *Wolfgang Amadeus Mozart*, translated by Clarence K. Pott, foreword by John Updike (Grand Rapids, MI: William B. Eerdmans Publishing Company, 1986), 27. The original German-language version of Barth's monograph was published in 1956 by Theologischer Verlag Zürich.

2. Shaw was writing specifically of the music Mozart gave to Sarastro in *The Magic Flute*. See Bernard Shaw, "Beethoven's Centenary," in *Shaw on Music*, ed. Eric Bentley (New York and Kent: Applause Books, 1995), 85.

3. Tovey, from his essay on Mozart's Symphony No. 40, K. 550, in *Essays in Musical Analysis: Symphonies and Other Orchestral Works* (Oxford: Oxford University Press, 1989), 440.

4. Barth, *Mozart*, 23.

5. Schubert cited in Maynard Solomon, *Mozart: A Life* (New York: Harper-Collins, 1995), 18. Wagner cited in Alfred Einstein, *Mozart: His Character, His Work*, trans. Arthur Mendel and Nathan Broder (New York and Oxford: Oxford University Press, 1945), 3.

6. "Heiterkeit ist sein hervorstechender Zug . . ." Ferruccio Busoni, *Von der Einheit der Musik: Verstreute Aufzeichnungen* (Berlin: Max Hesses Verlag, 1922), 79.

7. Einstein, *Mozart*, 471.

8. Barth, *Mozart*, 28.

9. Paul Henry Lang, *Music in Western Civilization* (New York: W. W. Norton, 1941), 674.

10. Barth, *Mozart*, 53.

11. Karol Berger also stresses the element of play in Mozart. See his chapter "Mozart at Play," in *Bach's Cycle, Mozart's Arrow: An Essay on the Origins of Musical Modernity* (Berkeley: University of California Press, 2007), 179–98.

12. Don Campbell, *The Mozart Effect: Tapping the Power of Music to Heal the Body, Strengthen the Mind, and Unlock the Creative Spirit* (New York: Avon Books, 1997).

13. Recent philosophical treatments of beauty include Alexander Nehamas, *Only a Promise of Happiness: The Place of Beauty in a World of Art* (Princeton, NJ: Princeton University Press, 2007), and Elaine Scarry, *On Beauty and Being Just* (Princeton, NJ: Princeton University Press, 1999).

14. Tovey refers to the passage from the very end of the slow introduction to Symphony No. 39, K. 543. See *Essays in Musical Analysis: Symphonies and Other Orchestral Works*, reprint ed. (Oxford: Oxford University Press, 1989), 435.

15. If along the way I refer to you, me, and others as "we," I do so in this invitational sense.

I: Beauty and Grace

1. Translation by A. S. Kline, copyright 2003. See http://tkline.pgcc.net/PITBR/German/Fausthome.htm.

2. I owe thanks to Mary Hunter for helping to articulate this point.

3. The use of E major also has much to contribute to this effect, being a rare key in the Mozart operas. It is worth noting that Mozart's other substantial E-major operatic number is the "calm seas" chorus in *Idomeneo*. My thanks to Jeffrey Gross for pointing out this connection.

4. Hermann Abert hears "languishing sensuous surrender" in these delayed cadences. Abert, W. A. *Mozart, Zweiter Teil: 1783–1791*, 7th ed. (Leipzig: Breitkopf & Härtel, 1956), 543.

5. Maynard Solomon, *Mozart: A Life* (New York: HarperCollins, 1995), 375.

6. "Aber das alles, so schön es sei, hat schon etwas von Bruchstück, von Auflösung in sich, ein Werk von so vollkommenem Guss ist seit dem Don Giovanni nicht mehr von Menschen gemacht worden." Hermann Hesse, *Der Steppenwolf* (Frankfurt am Main: Suhrkamp Taschenbuch, 1974), 262–63.

7. Barth, *Mozart*, 28.

8. Solomon, *Mozart*, 363.

9. Ferruccio Busoni once remarked on the songfulness of Mozart's music in all of its parts. See Busoni, "Zum Don Juan-Jubiläum: Ein kritischer Beitrag," in *Von der Einheit der Musik: Verstreute Aufzeichnungen* (Berlin: Max Hesses Verlag, 1922), 8.

10. And here I am thinking of an observation James Levine once made in an interview. When asked about the difference between conducting Wagner operas and conducting Mozart operas, he replied that whereas Wagner absorbs all your energy, leaving you drained, Mozart reflects your energy, leaving you energized.

11. William Hogarth, *The Analysis of Beauty*, edited with an introduction and notes by Ronald Paulson (New Haven, CT: Yale University Press, 1997), 54.

12. Ibid.

13. Ibid., 56.

14. Ibid.; see introduction, xli.

15. Ibid., 63–64.

16. David Bindman speaks of the "Line of Beauty" as "essentially a median form, at the point of balance between full curvilinearity and straightness." He goes on to infer a moral dimension to this construct, as thought poised between the extremes of self-display and self-effacement. See Bindman, *Hogarth and His Times* (Berkeley: University of California Press, 1997), 55. In this regard it is intriguing that the Line of Beauty on Hogarth's title page is closer to #5 in his figure 49 than to #4. One can also detect a tiny serpent's head on the title-page version. Not surprising, given the verse that Hogarth included just above this illustration, from Milton's *Paradise Lost*: "So vary'd he, and of his tortuous train / Curl'd many a wanton wreath, in sight of Eve, / To lure her eye." The seductive nature of

Mozart's beautiful musical lines will not be lost on Charles Rosen, as we shall discover below.

17. Rousseau, *Essai sur l'origine des langues*, chapter 13, "De la mélodie," in *Oeuvres complètes V: Écrits sur la musique, la langue et le théâtre* (Paris: Éditions Gallimard, 1995), 413. My thanks to Karol Berger for connecting this analogy to Rousseau.

18. Charles Rosen speaks frankly about the seductive nature of such passages, elevating this combination of the sensuous and the pure to a general condition of Mozart's music. See below, near the end of the present chapter.

19. I use this somewhat arcane term to refer to a chromatically altered note.

20. The passage confirms Edward Lowinsky's thesis about rhythmic motion in Mozart's melodies: that it typically intensifies as the melody continues, creating a subtle increase in energy. We encountered this as well in the very first example, from the Clarinet Concerto. Lowinsky, "On Mozart's Rhythm," *Musical Quarterly* 42, 2 (April 1956), 162–86.

21. A more complete treatise of this sort is provided by the Rondo in A Minor, K. 511, a rare opportunity to see Mozart write out melodic variants. For more on this and a number of other illuminating examples, see Robert Levin, "Improvised Embellishments in Mozart's Keyboard Music," *Early Music* 20, 2 (1992), 221–33.

22. Charles Rosen, *Critical Entertainments: Music Old and New* (Cambridge, MA: Harvard University Press, 2000), 101.

23. An astonishing contrapuntal dissonance awaits us somewhat later in this opening scene: see the discussion of this example in "Beautiful Dissonance," below.

24. Rosen, *The Classical Style: Haydn, Mozart, Beethoven*, expanded edition (New York: W.W. Norton, 1997), 324.

25. Ibid.

26. Ibid., 324–25.

27. Solomon, *Mozart*, 379.

II: Thresholds

1. Wye Jamison Allanbrook also tunes into the preternatural elements of this scene. After referring to the "gravely ticking triplets" that "measure out the precious seconds of life remaining to the Commendatore," she says this: "The very deliberateness of their ticking puts the scene out of time, for time passes normally only when attention is not called to it, leaving the shapes of events themselves to measure its passing for us." Allanbrook, *Rhythmic Gesture in Mozart: Le Nozze di Figaro and Don Giovanni* (Chicago and London: University of Chicago Press, 1983), 213.

2. Hermann Abert: "Es ist, als starrte uns ein verzerrtes Medusenantlitz an." Abert, *Mozart, Zweiter Teil*, 386.

3. This effect is due in part to the special presence of the bass voice in tonal music of this style. It is much more common to let the bass drop out than to let the rest of the harmony drop out.

4. For an illuminating exploration of the aesthetic and ethical aspects of

Giovanni's relation to modern temporality, see Karol Berger, *Bach's Cycle, Mozart's Arrow: An Essay on the Origins of Musical Modernity* (Berkeley: University of California Press, 2007), 262–63.

5. It was a pleasant, though somewhat uncanny, experience to encounter Abert's very similar description of this passage. His climax: "hier aber weht bereits die Luft der Ewigkeit, wo es kein Wünschen und Bangen mehr gibt, sondern nur ein unbewusstes Ahnen des göttlichen Geheimnisses." Also: "einer der überwältigendsten Partien in Mozarts gesamter Kunst. Sie beruht auf einer Sequenz von vier Gliedern, die aber nicht allein die Melodie, sondern den ganzen damit verbundenen Klangkomplex unaufhaltsam in die Tiefe zieht." Abert, *Mozart, Zweiter Teil*, 717.

6. See Christoph Wolff, *Mozart's Requiem: Historical and Analytical Studies, Documents, Score*, trans. Mary Whittall (Berkeley: University of California Press, 1994), 74–78.

7. Abert hears "hand wringing" in the violin syncopations here. *Mozart, Zweiter Teil*, 706.

8. These "fresh streams" are actually derived (through inversion and diminution) from the original "Requiem aeternam" theme. I am grateful to one of my astute anonymous readers for pointing this out.

9. It is illuminating to compare this to the setting of same text in Michael Haydn's C-minor Requiem, a piece Mozart knew and had consulted for his own Requiem—Haydn sets this same part of the text with a chorale melody in the chorus. See Wolff, *Mozart's Requiem*, 49.

10. The Kyrie movement of a standard mass cycle offers a ready opportunity for this same enclosure of tender lyricism within a more august structure: "Christe eleison," the plea to the Son, is more directly personal than "Kyrie eleison," the plea to God the Father. Mozart foregoes this opportunity in his Requiem, setting "Christe eleison" simultaneously with "Kyrie eleison" in a double fugue (perhaps because he had already staged such a contrast with the "Te decet"). But remember that in his well-known Mass in C Minor, K. 427, a solo soprano brings sheer lyric beauty to these words. See above, example 1.4.

11. Robert O. Gjerdingen, *Music in the Galant Style* (Oxford: Oxford University Press, 2007), 471.

12. I am grateful to Jonathan Cross for reminding me that the Requiem is often performed with boys' voices. In this case, the dichotomy I am reaching for here would be between woeful experience and hopeful innocence.

13. Although in the autograph manuscript Mozart clearly broke off after bar 8 of the Lacrymosa, Christoph Wolff argues that these eight bars are unlikely to be the very last music that Mozart composed for the Requiem. See Wolff, *Mozart's Requiem*, 29–32.

14. Alfred Einstein, *Mozart: His Character, His Work*, trans. Arthur Mendel and Nathan Broder (New York: Oxford University Press, 1945), 352.

15. The closing piece in Arnold Schoenberg's set of *Sechs kleine Klavierstücke*, op. 19, juxtaposes two similar sonorities (major sixth plus perfect fourth; two perfect fourths) to create the effect of a gently tolling bell.

16. For Robert Hatten, this move from a sharp-4 down to natural-4 can function as an expressive projection of the concept of abnegation. See Hatten, *Musi-*

cal Meaning in Beethoven: Markedness, Correlation, and Interpretation (Bloomington: Indiana University Press, 1994), 59.

17. The presence of a hymn text and the circumstance that most of the opening phrase behaves like a hymn setting with simple harmonies and minimal voice leading complicates our sense of the genre of *Ave verum corpus*. I have been calling *Ave verum corpus* a motet, but to what extent is it a hymn? The question was raised for me in provocative fashion by Laurence Dreyfus, and we concluded provisionally that if Mozart begins his motet as a hymn, it is only to transcend this more humble genre with the more imposing musical sophistication of the phrases to come.

18. The melodic *Gestalt* in bars 24–25 creates a parallelism with that of bars 5–6 from the first phrase: both passages pair an arcing soprano with a V–I progression, here in F, there in D. Bars 24–25 can thus be heard as an inward (i.e., flat-side) version of bars 5–6. I will say more about the potential identification of flat-side tonalities with inwardness in the section "Moving Inward."

19. A discussion with the ever insightful Dawna Lemaire was very helpful to me in articulating this point.

20. Christopher Matthay points out that when Mozart introduces a new theme at the beginning of a development, it is often in four-bar phrases that repeat up or down an octave. Such a theme then leads into the more animated "core" of the development (to use William Caplin's increasingly popular term, borrowed from Erwin Ratz). Matthay, "The Classical-Period Development Section: Compositional Strategies of Haydn, Mozart, Beethoven, and Schubert" (Ph.D. dissertation in progress, Princeton University).

21. Solomon treats such eruptions as a kind of expressive prototype in Mozart. See his *Mozart*, 187–90 (in the chapter entitled "Trouble in Paradise").

22. Schoenberg, *Theory of Harmony*, trans. Roy Carter (Berkeley: University of California Press, 1978), 324. Later in the treatise (p. 367), Schoenberg acknowledges that it is a passing harmony that goes by quickly. My thanks to Charles Carson for making me aware of Schoenberg's example, in a paper he wrote for a graduate seminar I conducted at the University of Pennsylvania in 2003.

23. Malcolm Bilson, from a remark after a colloquium talk, Cornell University, March 6, 2006.

24. I am reminded here of Robert Hatten's analysis of an expressive collapse in bar 5 of the slow movement of Beethoven's *Hammerklavier* Sonata, op. 106. See Hatten, *Musical Meaning in Beethoven*, 14–15.

25. The most striking of these, the B-flat pitted against the A, brings to mind a curious passage in the first movement of this sonata (bars 27–30), in which we hear B-flat rub against A four times in a row, three of them marked with *fp*. This digressive obsession—like scratching an itch—does not return in the recapitulation. But the theme from the finale scratches the same itch on the repetitive downbeats of its second and third bars.

26. This circumstance also raises the possibility that Mozart recomposed the return of his opening so as not to preempt the first loud augmented triad of the B section (G, B, D-sharp) with the selfsame sonority, a risk he does not run in the A section. His recomposition reaps other more obvious benefits, as will be discussed below.

27. "For a piece of such short duration, there are too many disparate melodic and contrapuntal devices. The texture changes too frequently and too suddenly." Thus wrote Ernst Oster, in a trenchant analysis of this Minuet. Pointing to various perceived compositional flaws, Oster concludes that this piece falls into one of Mozart's more experimental periods (ca. 1782 in this case). See Oster, "A Schenkerian View," part of an analytical symposium on the K. 355 (K. 576b) Minuet in Maury Yeston, ed., *Readings in Schenker Analysis and Other Approaches* (New Haven and London: Yale University Press, 1977), 123.

28. The lines of this passage move just slowly enough that one can hear fascinating verticalities emerge from the subtly shifting linear figures—as Gottfried Weber was at pains to point out, in a famous nineteenth-century analysis of this opening, where he parsed the passage "chord" by "chord." An annotated translation of Weber's analysis is available in Ian Bent, ed. and trans., *Music Analysis in the Nineteenth Century, Volume 1: Fugue, Form and Style* (Cambridge: Cambridge University Press, 1994), 157–83.

29. See note 39 below, regarding Robert Gjerdingen's view of the passage in K. 467.

30. The bell-like core of this sonority is formed by the pitches B-flat, C, and G. One of my anonymous readers ingeniously suggests a common voice-leading pattern that is subject to displacement here, involving the ascent from C to D to E-flat taking place underneath the descent of G to F to E-flat.

31. I am grateful to James Webster for profiling this tension between the horizontal and the vertical in response to an early version of this discussion of dissonance in Mozart (at Cornell University, on March 6, 2006).

32. For a fascinating application of this idea to Beethoven's heroic style, see David B. Greene, *Temporal Processes in Beethoven's Music* (New York: Gordon and Breach, 1982), 18–19.

33. In this regard, see also Leonard Ratner's definition of sonata form, in *Classic Music: Expression, Form, and Style* (New York: Schirmer Books, 1980), 246.

34. Maynard Solomon, at the outset one of his chapters on Mozart's beautiful music ("Fearful Symmetries"), speaks of the "excruciating, surplus quality that transforms loveliness into ecstasy, grace into sublimity, pleasure into rapture." Solomon, *Mozart*, 363.

35. Throughout much of the same chapter (ibid., 372–82), Solomon discusses the strangeness of beauty in Mozart, with reference to a range of aesthetic observations, from Plotinus to Freud. This chapter, taken together with the chapters "Trouble in Paradise" and "The Power of Music," forms a compact and brilliant treatise on the interrelated aesthetic and ethical dimensions of Mozart's music.

36. George Santayana, *The Sense of Beauty: Being the Outline of Aesthetic Theory* (New York: Dover Publications, 1955), 164.

37. Abert, *Mozart, Zweiter Teil*, 14.

38. For a stimulating treatment of Mozart as a transitional figure between the Enlightenment focus on object and the Romantic focus on subject, see Denis Donoghue, "Approaching Mozart," in James M. Morris, ed., *On Mozart* (Cambridge: University of Cambridge Press, 1994), 33–35.

39. See the foregoing discussion of this passage in "Beautiful Dissonance," above. In a personal communication regarding these bars, Robert Gjerdingen observed that two different kinds of patterns—the upper-voice sequence, and the harmonic exchange over the pedal point—operate in a kind of oblique counterpoint, which helps lend the passage its special aura.

40. Charles Rosen has claimed that "No composer was a greater master of the expansion of the center of a phrase than Mozart." See Rosen, *The Classical Style: Haydn, Mozart, Beethoven* (New York: Norton, 1971; 1997), 88.

41. Rudolph Otto, *The Idea of the Holy: an Inquiry into the Non-Rational Factor in the Idea of the Divine and Its Relation to the Rational*, trans. John W. Harvey (Oxford: Oxford University Press, 1923; 1973), 126. Otto's phrase first came to my attention in Richard A. Etlin's book *In Defense of Humanism: Value in the Arts and Letters* (Cambridge: Cambridge University Press, 1996), 154.

42. E.T.A. Hoffmann, review of Beethoven's Fifth Symphony, in *E.T.A. Hoffmann's Musical Writings: "Kreisleriana," "The Poet and the Composer," Music Criticism*, ed. David Charlton, trans. Martyn Clarke (Cambridge: Cambridge University Press, 1989), 237–38.

43. Tovey borrows this term from Horace. For the original context of "purple patches," see Horace, *Ars Poetica*, lines 14–16, in which Horace deplores the tendency of poets to pad their works by cobbling together ill-assorted purple patches of descriptive splendor. For Tovey's much more positive use of the term, see "Haydn's Chamber Music," in *The Mainstream of Music and Other Essays* (New York: Oxford University Press, 1949), 19.

44. Often, as in the excerpts from the slow movements of K. 550 and K. 516, the purple patch sets up the definitive cadence in the so-called second theme group. Tovey, "Haydn's Chamber Music," 19, relegates the "purple patch" exclusively to this section of the form. Other interesting examples include the first movement of the Piano Trio in E Major, K. 542 (bars 74–83); or the finale of the String Quartet in C Major, K. 465 (bars 89–100); or the playful example from the finale of the String Quintet in C Major, K. 515 (bars 120–34).

These interpolations, each involving the flat-six sonority, help make the eventual cadence in the dominant key unimpeachable, and not just because a zone of tonal uncertainty gets swept away by tonal confirmation, or because the flat-six marks the dominant key's dominant so unequivocally. Rather this practice also allows the new key, the dominant, access to an internal history, to enhanced experience and depth. And by dipping into the flat side of the dominant key, this process arguably allows the key of the dominant to be confirmed through a tonal process that in some sense passes back through the neighborhood of the original tonic (located on the circle of fifths one step flat-wise from the dominant key). The result is a dominant key area with history, a dominant more deeply rooted in the tonal psychology of the movement.

45. Gary Tomlinson, *Metaphysical Song: An Essay on Opera* (Princeton, NJ: Princeton University Press, 1999), 77.

46. Karol Berger, *A Theory of Art* (New York: Oxford University Press, 2000), 136.

47. Ibid.

48. Cited in Berger, *Theory of Art*, 208. From G.W.F. Hegel, *Aesthetics: Lectures on Fine Art*, 2 vols., trans. T. M. Knox (Oxford: Oxford University Press, 1975), 902.

49. Marshall Brown, "Mozart and After: The Revolution in Musical Consciousness," *Critical Inquiry* 7 (1980–81), 689–706.

50. "Frequently . . . in mature Mozart the greatest beauties exist in brief compass, concentrated in fleeting, self-contained passages whose overwhelming effect is magnified by their unexpected emergence and subsidence into a less rapturous context. . . . Such moments wait to be discovered: they are transitional, passing references to pure beauty, captured for an instant before they sink back into the relatively quotidian." Maynard Solomon, in *Mozart*, 370.

51. This notion was brought home to me with particular force in a stunning recent exhibition at the Metropolitan Museum of Art ("Rooms with a View: The Open Window in the 19th Century," which ran from April 5 to July 4, 2011). The exhibition featured drawings and paintings from the first half of the century, by a range of European artists who had been inspired by two sepia drawings Friedrich produced ca. 1805. A similar relation to the outside world can be seen in Romantic landscape paintings, especially those of Friedrich. In many of these, a *Rückenfigur* appears to concentrate subjectivity, facing a landscape composed more as a vision than as a realistic natural scene.

52. Rose Rosengard Subotnik, in an essay originally written in 1982, explicitly tied structural disjunctions in Mozart's last three symphonies to an incipient worldview that critiques Enlightenment reason. Hers is a pioneering account, a characteristically rich and thoughtful treatment of music as a crucial strand of humanistic thought. See "Evidence of a Critical Worldview in Mozart's Last Three Symphonies," in *Developing Variations: Style and Ideology in Western Music* (Minneapolis: University of Minnesota Press, 1991), 98–111.

53. I have explored this idea at much greater length in "Mozart's *felix culpa*: *Così fan tutte* and the Irony of Beauty," *Musical Quarterly* 78, 1 (Spring 1994), 77–98.

54. Hunter also traces the existence of a Viennese opera buffa convention calling for a specific type of musical beauty, in which "beautiful music becomes a dramatic agent in its own right." This convention is often employed as a sign of liminal interiority, as in Hunter's telling examples from Haydn's *Il mondo della luna* and Mozart's *Così fan tutte*. See Mary Hunter, *The Culture of Opera Buffa in Mozart's Vienna: A Poetics of Entertainment* (Princeton, NJ: Princeton University Press, 1999), especially 285–96.

55. As, for example, in the aftermath of the Commendatore's death in act 1 of Don Giovanni, discussed above, example 2.1. Another potent example from *Don Giovanni* is the discovery of Leporello masquerading as Giovanni, in the sextet from act 2, scene 8.

56. It is likely no coincidence that the modern listening experience is so often solitary. In the words of Joseph Kerman, "today's solitary listening seems a return to or, rather, an apotheosis of the Romantic ideal of self-consciousness modeled in music, celebrated by figures such as Tieck, E.T.A. Hoffmann, and Schopenhauer." Kerman, *Concerto Conversations* (Cambridge, MA: Harvard University Press, 1999), 125.

III: Grace and Renewal

1. Cuthbert Girdlestone heard it as an incomplete question, with a presence like that of "an inscription carved over a portal and repeated at intervals inside the building." Joseph Kerman calls it a proposition, "balancing two senses of the word, that of proposal and that of invitation." For Charles Rosen, it is a "frame" for the form, for Susan McClary, Elaine Sisman, and Richard Taruskin, a "motto." See Cuthbert Girdlestone, *Mozart and his Piano Concertos* (Norman: University of Oklahoma Press, 1952), 247; Joseph Kerman, "Interpreting Mozart's K. 453" (unpublished discussion paper for a colloquium, shared by author); Charles Rosen, *Classical Style*, 223; Susan McClary, "A Dialectic from the Enlightenment: Mozart's Piano Concerto in G Major, K. 453, Movement 2," *Cultural Critique* 4 (1986), 141; Elaine Sisman, *Mozart: The "Jupiter" Symphony*, Cambridge Music Handbooks (Cambridge: Cambridge University Press, 1993), 60; Richard Taruskin, *The Oxford History of Western Music, Vol. 2: The Seventeenth and Eighteenth Centuries* (Oxford: Oxford University Press, 2005), 613.

2. Rosen, *Classical Style*, 223.

3. Robert Winter, "The Bifocal Close and the Evolution of the Viennese Classical Style," *Journal of the American Musicological Society*, 42, 2 (Summer 1989), 275–337.

4. In terms of concerto form, we have just experienced the end of the solo exposition, such that the "new theme" that follows takes place in a developmental space. My thanks to one of my anonymous readers for collating my discussion with various important aspects of concerto form.

5. Leonard G. Ratner, *Classic Music: Expression, Form, and Style* (New York: Schirmer Books, 1980), 225–27.

6. " . . . as if solving a chess problem in four moves," in Richard Taruskin's apt description of Mozart's procedure here—apt not only because of the move-by-move nature of this transition, but also because the simile draws on another notable area of human intellection whose mastery involves stunning ellipses of reasoning, in which miles of combinatorial possibilities are bridged instantly. Taruskin, *Oxford History of Music*, vol. 2, 618.

7. The articulated final eighth note in each of the four bars of transition provides a subtle forecast of the similar eighth note at the end of the first bar of the refrain.

8. Sisman, *"Jupiter" Symphony*, 60.

9. Compare Susan McClary's description of the refrain: "Formally it seems, on the one hand (partly because of the simplicity of its syntax), to convey a sense of sublime certainty and inexorability. Yet, on the other hand, it is open-ended and in need of an answer (or consequent phrase) if it is to attain closure." McClary, "Dialectic from the Enlightenment," 144.

10. Even with this tonic completion, the opening utterance does not behave like a fully conventional period, for it fails to pause on the half cadence.

11. I pursue these thoughts in "The Second Nature of Sonata Form," in *Music Theory and Natural Order*, Suzannah Clark and Alexander Rehding, eds. (Cambridge: Cambridge University Press, 2001), 111–41, and reprinted in Scott Burnham, *Sounding Values: Selected Essays* (Aldershot: Ashgate Press, 2010), 155–85.

12. The most extended, insightful, and imaginative treatment of Mozart's re-transitions is by Roman Ivanovitch, who is interested in idealized retransitions that "can console, restore or transport." In particular, Ivanovitch focuses on "a type of retransition procedure, quintessentially expressed in slow movements, involving a contrapuntally braided linear descent over a dominant pedal. This gesture gives rise to some of the most exalted moments in all of Mozart." I am grateful to Ivanovitch for allowing me access to a proof copy of his article, which appears as "Mozart's Art of Retransition," in *Music Analysis* 30, 1 (2011), 1–36.

13. My thanks to one of my anonymous readers for convincingly insisting on such a hearing of this recapitulation.

14. For a Schenkerian calibration of this space between V/vi and the returning tonic, see David Beach, "A Recurring Pattern in Mozart's Music," *Journal of Music Theory* 27 (1983), 1–29.

15. Roman Ivanovitch, "Recursive/Discursive: Variation and Sonata in the Andante of Mozart's String Quartet in F, K.590," *Music Theory Spectrum* 32, 2 (2010), 155.

16. Charles Rosen cites this retransition as a brilliant example of avoiding the cadence on the submediant. Rosen, *Sonata Forms*, rev. ed. (New York: W. W. Norton, 1988), 270–71.

17. Rosen, *Classical Style*, 49.

18. Rosen again: "Mozart's most breathtaking uses of the [falling-fifth] sequence are at the ends of his developments: we sense that the tonic is about to reappear, and with the conviction that Mozart's sense of proportion conveys, we often know in just how many measures, and yet we are led to it by a sequence richly worked out with a felicity of detail that makes us half forget the inevitability of the larger action, or sense it in our pulse while we are dazzled by what appears to be ornament and is really a heightening of the dramatic form." Ibid., p. 49.

19. A discussion of this stunning retransition could also find a home in the above section on "Beautiful Dissonance." One of my anonymous readers brilliantly observed that every eighth-note beat is dissonant in this passage!

20. We've already encountered a striking version of this kind of thinking within the Andante to K. 453, where Mozart moves from the dominant of C-sharp to the dominant of C.

21. Allanbrook, "Two Threads through the Labyrinth: Topic and Process in the First Movements of K. 332 and K. 333," in Wye Jamison Allanbrook, Janet M. Levy, and William Mahrt, eds, *Convention in Eighteenth-and Nineteenth-Century Music: Essays in Honor of Leonard G. Ratner* (Stuyvesant, NY: Pendragon Press, 1992), 145–46.

22. For a superb treatment of the sublime and the learned in this movement and the entire "Jupiter" Symphony, see Elaine Sisman, *Mozart: The "Jupiter" Symphony.*

23. Wye Jamison Allanbrook, *Rhythmic Gesture in Mozart: Le Nozze di Figaro and Don Giovanni* (Chicago: University of Chicago Press, 1983), 324.

24. For Leonard Ratner, "this passage incorporates a musical cartoon, sketched in three treble lines, a caricature of weighty chromatic passages heard

earlier in Act II. The style of the passage is frankly *buffa*." Ratner, "Mozart's Parting Gifts," *Journal of Musicology* 18, 1 (2001), 191.

25. Allanbrook, "Mozart's Tunes and the Comedy of Closure," in James M. Morris, ed., *On Mozart* (Cambridge: Woodrow Wilson Center Press and Cambridge University Press, 1994), 186.

26. The sixteenth notes here are perhaps reminiscent of the repeating eighth-note figures in the Trio section, which appear in the phrase after the passage discussed above. If so, it is as though the memory of those warming eighths helps push away from the Adagio minor into the Allegro major.

27. Allanbrook, "Comic Issues in Mozart's Piano Concertos," in Neal Zaslaw, ed., *Mozart's Piano Concertos: Text, Context, Interpretation* (Ann Arbor: University of Michigan Press, 1996), 85.

28. Martin Geck, *Mozart: Eine Biographie* (Reinbek bei Hamburg: Rowohlt, 2006), 216.

29. This section also represents the first disruption of the prevailing 32-bar sections (8 × 2 twice) of the variation structure. We've just heard the theme and five variations, for a total of 6 × 32 bars (192 bars; because of repeat signs in the theme and first variation we are at bar 160). With this in mind, it is worth pointing out that the succeeding "finale of the finale" is 175 bars long—less than 20 bars shy of the entire movement up to this point (but of course at a faster tempo).

Knowing Innocence

1. As in this 1985 testimonial, from no less than Cardinal Joseph Ratzinger, before he became the pope: "For me, the greatness of [Mozart's] music is the most immediate and manifest verification that history offers us of the Christian image of humankind and the Christian belief in redemption. Whoever is truly struck by [this music] knows in his innermost being that the creed is the truth, even if he still requires many steps to fulfill this insight with understanding and will." ("Die Größe dieser Musik ist für mich die unmittelbarste und evidenteste Verifikation des christlichen Menschenbildes und des christlichen Erlösungsglaubens, die uns die Geschichte anbietet. Wer wirklich von ihr getroffen wird, weiß irgendwie vom Innersten her, dass der Glaube wahr ist, auch wenn er noch so viele Schritte braucht, um diese Einsicht mit Verstand und Willen nachzuvollziehen."). Cited by Cardinal Christoph Schönborn, Sermon at St. Peter's, Rome, November 19, 2006 (http://www.erzdioezese-wien.at/content/artikel/a11841).

2. Karl Barth makes a similar statement: "It is . . . just this stopping short of extremes, just this wise confrontation and mixture of the elements which . . . are the constituents of that freedom with which Mozart's music renders the true *vox humana* through the whole scale of its possibilities." Barth, *Mozart*, 54.

3. For a more philosophically rich account of Mozart's implicit critique of Enlightenment values, see Subotnik, "Evidence of a Critical Worldview in Mozart's Last Three Symphonies."

4. Roman Ivanovitch offers a richly appointed treatment of such passages, undertaken from a different theoretical perspective, in "Recursive/Discursive: Variation and Sonata in the Andante of Mozart's String Quartet in F, K. 590,"

Music Theory Spectrum 32, 2 (Fall 2010). On p. 150 of this article Ivanovitch talks about how one such passage "is actually staged to sound parenthetical, to offer itself as distinct from its surroundings: an enclave or oasis—a lyrical reverie."

5. As Barth puts it: "No laughter without tears, no weeping without laughter!" Barth, *Mozart*, p. 54.

6. Mary Hunter, discussing the "unbelievably gorgeous music" in various scenes of *Così fan tutte*, argues that this musical beauty is an essential part of the dramaturgy, in part because such scenes "crystallize the eternally ambiguous relation between sympathy and ridicule that is one of the opera's principal topics." Hunter, *The Culture of Opera Buffa in Mozart's Vienna*, 287.

7. Barth, *Mozart*, 55.

8. Berger, *Bach's Cycle, Mozart's Arrow*, 8.

9. As noted in my earlier discussion of retransitions (after example 3.9), Charles Rosen points out that circle-of-fifths progressions often have the effect of "treading water" in the Classical style, whereas such progressions usually provide primary locomotion in the Baroque style. See Rosen, *The Classical Style*, especially pp. 49 and 58.

10. Thanks to Mary Hunter for stressing the particulars of this floating texture.

11. I treat the notion of ironic beauty as a loss of innocence with reference to *Così fan tutte* in "Mozart's *felix culpa* : *Così fan tutte* and the Irony of Beauty," *Musical Quarterly* 78, 1 (1994).

BIBLIOGRAPHY

Abert, Hermann. *W. A. Mozart, Zweiter Teil: 1783–1791*. 7th ed. Leipzig: Breit-kopf & Härtel, 1956.

Allanbrook, Wye Jamison. "Comic Issues in Mozart's Piano Concertos." In *Mozart's Piano Concertos: Text, Context, Interpretation*, edited by Neal Zaslaw, 75–105. Ann Arbor: University of Michigan Press, 1996.

———. "Mozart's Tunes and the Comedy of Closure." In *On Mozart*, edited by James M. Morris, 169–86. Cambridge: Cambridge University Press, 1994.

———. *Rhythmic Gesture in Mozart: Le Nozze di Figaro and Don Giovanni*. Chicago and London: University of Chicago Press, 1983.

———. "Two Threads through the Labyrinth: Topic and Process in the First Movements of K. 332 and K. 333." In *Convention in Eighteenth- and Nineteenth-Century Music: Essays in Honor of Leonard G. Ratner*, edited by W. J. Allanbrook, J. Levy, and W. Mahrt, 125–72. Stuyvesant, NY: Pendragon Press, 1992.

Barth, Karl. *Wolfgang Amadeus Mozart*. Translated Clarence K. Pott, Foreword by John Updike. Grand Rapids, MI: William B. Eerdmans Publishing Company, 1986.

Beach, David. "A Recurring Pattern in Mozart's Music." *Journal of Music Theory* 27, no. 1 (Spring 1983): 1–29.

Berger, Karol. *Bach's Cycle, Mozart's Arrow: An Essay on the Origins of Musical Modernity*. Berkeley: University of California Press, 2007.

———. *A Theory of Art*. New York: Oxford University Press, 2000.

Bindman, David. *Hogarth and His Times*. Berkeley: University of California Press, 1997.

Brown, Marshall. "Mozart and After: The Revolution in Musical Consciousness." *Critical Inquiry* 7 (1980–81): 689–706.

Burnham, Scott. "Mozart's *felix culpa*: *Così fan tutte* and the Irony of Beauty." *Musical Quarterly* 78, no. 1 (Spring 1994): 77–98.

———. "The Second Nature of Sonata Form." In *Music Theory and Natural Order*, edited by S. Clark and A. Rehding, 111–41. Cambridge: Cambridge University Press, 2001.

———. *Sounding Values: Selected Essays*. Aldershot: Ashgate Press, 2010.

Busoni, Ferruccio. *Von der Einheit der Musik: Verstreute Aufzeichnungen*. Leipzig: Max Hesses Verlag, 1922.

Campbell, Don. *The Mozart Effect: Tapping the Power of Music to Heal the Body, Strengthen the Mind, and Unlock the Creative Spirit*. New York: Avon Books, 1997.

Donoghue, Denis. "Approaching Mozart." In *On Mozart*, edited by James M. Morris, 15–35. Cambridge: University of Cambridge Press, 1994.

Einstein, Alfred. *Mozart: His Character, His Work.* Translated by Arthur Mendel and Nathan Broder. New York, Oxford: Oxford University Press, 1945.

Eisen, Cliff and Sadie, Stanley. *The New Grove Mozart.* London: Macmillan, 2002.

Etlin, Richard A. *In Defense of Humanism: Value in the Arts and Letters.* Cambridge: Cambridge University Press, 1996.

Geck, Martin. *Mozart: Eine Biographie.* Reinbek bei Hamburg: Rowohlt, 2006.

Girdlestone, Cuthbert. *Mozart and His Piano Concertos.* Norman: University of Oklahoma Press, 1952.

Gjerdingen, Robert O. *Music in the Galant Style.* Oxford: Oxford University Press, 2007.

Greene, David B. *Temporal Processes in Beethoven's Music.* New York: Gordon and Breach, 1982.

Hatten, Robert. *Musical Meaning in Beethoven: Markedness, Correlation, and Interpretation.* Bloomington: Indiana University Press, 1994.

Hegel, Georg Wilhelm Friedrich. *Aesthetics: Lectures on Fine Art.* 2 vols. Translated by T. M. Knox. Oxford: Oxford University Press, 1975.

Hildesheimer, Wolfgang. *Mozart.* Frankfurt am Main: Suhrkamp, 1980.

Hoffmann, E. T. A. *E .T. A. Hoffmann's Musical Writings: "Kreisleriana," "The Poet and the Composer," Music Criticism.* Edited by David Charlton. Translated by Martyn Clarke. Cambridge: Cambridge University Press, 1989.

Hogarth, William. *The Analysis of Beauty.* Edited with introduction and notes by Ronald Paulson. New Haven: Yale University Press, 1997.

Hunter, Mary. *The Culture of Opera Buffa in Mozart's Vienna: A Poetics of Entertainment.* Princeton, NJ: Princeton University Press, 1999.

Ivanovitch, Roman. "Mozart's Art of Retransition." *Music Analysis* 30, no. 1 (2011): 1-36.

———. "Recursive/Discursive: Variation and Sonata in the Andante of Mozart's String Quartet in F, K. 590." *Music Theory Spectrum* 32, no. 2 (2010): 145–64.

Kerman, Joseph. *Concerto Conversations.* Cambridge, MA: Harvard University Press, 1999.

Levin, Robert. "Improvised Embellishments in Mozart's Keyboard Music." *Early Music* 20, no. 2 (1992): 221–33.

Lowinsky, Edward. "On Mozart's Rhythm." *Musical Quarterly*, 42, no. 2 (April 1956): 162–86.

Matthay, Christopher. "The Classical-Period Development Section: Compositional Strategies of Haydn, Mozart, Beethoven, and Schubert." Ph.D. dissertation in progress, Princeton University.

McClary, Susan. "A Dialectic from the Enlightenment: Mozart's Piano Concerto in G Major, K. 453, Movement 2." *Cultural Critique* 4 (1986): 129–69.

Nehamas, Alexander. *Only a Promise of Happiness: The Place of Beauty in a World of Art.* Princeton, NJ: Princeton University Press, 2007.

Oster, Ernst. "Analysis Symposium on Mozart, Menuetto K.V. 355: A Schenkerian View." In *Readings in Schenker Analysis and Other Approaches*, edited by Maury Yeston, 121–40. New Haven and London: Yale University Press, 1977.

Otto, Rudolph. *The Idea of the Holy: an Inquiry into the Non-Rational Factor in the Idea of the Divine and Its Relation to the Rational.* Translated by John W. Harvey. Oxford: Oxford University Press, 1923; 1973.

Ratner, Leonard. *Classic Music: Expression, Form, and Style.* New York: Schirmer Books, 1980.

———. "Mozart's Parting Gifts," *Journal of Musicology* 18, no. 1 (2001): 189–212.

Rosen, Charles. *The Classical Style: Haydn, Mozart, Beethoven.* Expanded ed. New York: W.W. Norton, 1997.

———. *Critical Entertainments: Music Old and New.* Cambridge, MA: Harvard University Press, 2000.

———. *Sonata Forms.* Rev. ed. New York: W. W. Norton, 1988.

Rousseau, Jean-Jacques. "Essai sur l'origine des langues." In *Oeuvres complètes V: Écrits sur la musique, la langue et le théâtre.* Paris: Éditions Gallimard, 1995.

Santayana, George. *The Sense of Beauty: Being the Outline of Aesthetic Theory.* New York: Dover Publications, 1955.

Scarry, Elaine. *On Beauty and Being Just.* Princeton, NJ: Princeton University Press, 1999.

Schoenberg, Arnold. *Theory of Harmony.* Translated by Roy Carter. Berkeley: University of California Press, 1978.

Shaw, Bernard. "Beethoven's Centenary." In *Shaw on Music*, edited by Eric Bentley, 83–88. New York, Kent: Applause Books, 1995.

Sisman, Elaine. *Mozart: The "Jupiter" Symphony.* Cambridge Music Handbooks. Cambridge: Cambridge University Press, 1993.

Solomon, Maynard. *Mozart: A Life.* New York: HarperCollins, 1995.

Subotnik, Rose Rosengard. *Developing Variations: Style and Ideology in Western Music.* Minneapolis: University of Minnesota Press, 1991.

Taruskin, Richard. *The Oxford History of Western Music, Vol. 2: The Seventeenth and Eighteenth Centuries.* Oxford: Oxford University Press, 2005.

Tomlinson, Gary. *Metaphysical Song: An Essay on Opera.* Princeton, NJ: Princeton University Press, 1999.

Tovey, Donald Francis. *Essays in Musical Analysis: Symphonies and Other Orchestral Works.* Oxford: Oxford University Press, 1989.

———. *The Mainstream of Music and Other Essays.* New York: Oxford University Press, 1949.

Weber, Gottfried. "A Particularly Remarkable Passage in a String Quartet in C by Mozart." In *Music Analysis in the Nineteenth Century, Volume 1: Fugue, Form and Style*, edited and translated by Ian Bent, 157–83. Cambridge: Cambridge University Press, 1994.

Winter, Robert. "The Bifocal Close and the Evolution of the Viennese Classical Style." *Journal of the American Musicological Society* 42, no. 2 (Summer 1989): 275–337.

Wolff, Christoph. *Mozart's Requiem: Historical and Analytical Studies, Documents, Score.* Translated by Mary Whittall. Berkeley: University of California Press, 1994.

INDEX

Abert, Hermann, 101, 172n4, 173n2, 174n5, 174n7
Allanbrook, Wye Jamison, 139, 143–45, 148, 158, 173n1
Amadeus, 22 144

Babes in Toyland, 148
Bach, Johann Sebastian, 1, 3
Barth, Karl, 1, 2, 18–19, 166, 181n2, 182n5
Beach, David, 180n14
Beauty: as aesthetic category, 4; and becoming grace, 21; as ironic intimation, 115; as special property of consciousness, 168; strange, 36; in suspension, 7–18
Beethoven, Ludwig van, 109, 128, 166; and Symphony No. 3, "Eroica," Op. 55, 40, 81, 82–83, 88–89, 128
Bent, Ian, 176n28
Berger, Karol, 114, 171n11, 173n17, 174n4; and *Bach's Cycle, Mozart's Arrow*, 167
Bifocal close, 120
Bilson, Malcolm, 88
Bindman, David, 172n16
Boulez, Pierre, 81
Brown, Marshall, 114
Busoni, Ferruccio, 1, 172n9

Campbell, Don, 171n12
Caplin, William, 175n20
Carson, Charles, 175n22
Catholicism, Baroque, 64
Christ, figure of, 69, 73, 75
Christianity: and concept of redemption, 75, 165
Christological narrative, 165
Closure: in Classical-style music, 143; in Mozart's music, 143–64
Communion, ritual of, 73
Consciousness: altered, 114, 115; and

beauty, 168; ironic self-consciousness, 5, 167–68
"Corelli leapfrog," 64
Cross, Jonathan, 174n12

Dionysian frenzy: in Mozart's music, 80
Dissonance, 80–101; as aesthetic presence, 91–92; contrapuntal, 77, 80; etymology of, 101; as intimation, 100; and ironic self-consciousness, 100; out-of-phase, 93, 95; as surplus, 100
Don Giovanni: as Don Juan figure, 46–48
Donoghue, Denis, 176n38
Don Quixote, 168
Dreyfus, Laurence, 175n17

Einstein, Alfred, 2, 69
Enlightenment thought, 5, 101, 165–66, 176n38; and Classical-style music, 100
Eruptions: in Mozart's music, 76–80
Etlin, Richard A., 177n41
Expressivity: in melodic lines, 30–35

Flat-side harmony: as sign of interiority, 103–4, 108–9
Friedrich, Caspar David: and *The Woman in the Window*, 115

Geck, Martin, 158
Girdlestone, Cuthbert, 179n1
Gjerdingen, Robert, 64, 176n29, 177n39
Goethe, Johann Wolfgang von, 7, 66
Grace: as *Anmut*, 7, 142; as *Gnade*, 142
Gratitude, 169
Greene, David B., 176n32
Gross, Jeffrey, 172n3

Handel, George Frederic: and Funeral Anthem, 55–56
Hatten, Robert, 174n16, 175n24
Haydn, Franz Joseph, 103, 128, 166

Haydn, Michael: and Requiem in G minor, 174n9
Hegel, Georg Wilhelm Friedrich, 114
Hesse, Hermann: and *Steppenwolf,* 18
Hoffmann, E. T. A., 102–3, 114, 166
Hogarth, William: and *Analysis of Beauty,* 20–22, 29; and Line of Beauty, Line of Grace, 21
Horace: and *Ars Poetica,* 177n43
Hunter, Mary, 115, 172n2, 182n6, 182n10

Innocence: and "knowing," 5, 22; loss of, 116; renewable, 116, 164, 165
Interiority: and music, 101–16; and transcendence, 114
Irony, 168; and intimation, 115 (*see also* Consciousness: ironic self-consciousness)
Ivanovitch, Roman, 132, 180n12, 181n4

Kant, Immanuel, 114, 167
Kerman, Joseph, 178n56, 179n1
Kierkegaard, Søren, 36
Kleist, Heinrich von: and "On the Marionette Theater," 166

Lang, Paul Henry, 2
Lemaire, Dawna, 175n19
Levin, Robert, 173n21
Levine, James, 172n10
Lieto fine, 144
Liminal effects: in Mozart's music, 37–116
Lowinsky, Edward, 173n20

Matthay, Christopher, 175n20
McClary, Susan, 179n1, 179n9
Medusa, 41
Melody: as analogue to drawn line, 21; in Mozart's music, 19–35
Mephistopheles, 168
Metropolitan Museum of Art, 178n51
Milton, John: and *Paradise Lost,* 172n16
Mozart, Wolfgang Amadeus: and closure, 143–64; and compositional freedom, 2, 158, 167; and dissonance, 80–101; and divinity, 1, 2, 19; and frenzy, 76–80; as Harlequin, 158; and innocence, 165–69; and instrumentation, 19; and lightness, 164, 166; and melody, 19–35; musical judgment of, 2, 165; and obliquity, 167; and the "open close," 164; and perfection, 1, 18; and play, 2; and rhythmic freedom, 167; sacred music of, 48–75;

and sensuous pleasure, 34–36; "sound of," 2, 7; and the supernatural, 37–48; and thematic returns, 117–42
Mozart, Wolfgang Amadeus: works of, *Ave verum corpus,* K. 618, 68–75, 165
Clarinet Concerto in A, K. 622, 7–11, 167
Così fan tutte, K. 588, 11, 105, 115; and "Soave sia il vento," 11–18, 105, 167
Don Giovanni, 18, 35–36, 68, 143–44, 163, 178n55; Act 2, Finale of, 143–46; Act 1, Scene 1 of, 37–42; Overture of, 40–47
Fantasia in C minor, K. 475, 78–80
Mass in C minor, K. 427, Kyrie, 21–23, 174n10
Minuet for Piano, K. 576b, 92–94
Piano Concerto 17 in G, K. 453: Allegretto (Finale) of, 158–63; Andante of, 117–28, 180n20
Piano Concerto 20 in D minor, K. 466, 144–51
Piano Concerto 21 in C, K. 467, 31–35, 97, 101–3, 105
Piano Concerto 27 in B-flat, K. 595, 26–30
Piano Sonata in A minor, K. 310, 76–78, 80
Piano Sonata in B-flat, K. 333, 84–85, 90
Piano Sonata in F, K. 280, 131–32
Piano Sonata in F, K. 332, 30–31, 139
Piano Sonata in F, K. 533, 86–92, 94
Piano Trio in E, K. 542, 177n44
Requiem, K. 626: and Confutatis, 48–55, 65–67; and Dies Irae, 67; and Introitus, 55–64; and Lacrymosa, 68; and Recordare, 64–65, 67; and Rex tremendae, 64, 67; and Tuba mirum, 67
Rondo in A minor, K. 511, 173n21
Serenade for Twelve Winds and String Bass, K. 361, 22–26
String Quartet in C, "Dissonant," K. 465: Allegro (Finale) of, 177n44; Adagio of, 95, 114
String Quintet in C, K. 515, 177n44
String Quintet in D, K. 593, 134–39
String Quintet in E-flat, K. 614, 97–100
String Quintet in G minor, K. 516: Adagio-Allegro (Finale) of, 150–60; Adagio ma non troppo of, 105–8, 155–56, 177n44; Allegro of, 153–55; Menuetto of, 154–56

Symphony 29 in A, K. 201, 19–20
Symphony 39 in E-flat, K. 543, 81–87, 132–33, 136
Symphony 40 in G minor, K. 550: Allegro molto of, 80–81, 85, 128–31; Andante of, 95–97, 104–5, 114, 132–34, 177n44
Symphony 41 in C, K. 551: Andante cantabile of, 108–13, 132, 135; Molto Allegro (Finale) of, 139–43
Vesperae Solennes de Confessore, K. 339: and "Laudate Dominum," 168–69
"Mozart Effect," 3

Nehamas, Alexander, 171n13
Noumenon, 114–16

Oster, Ernst, 176n27
Otto, Rudolph, 102
Out-of-phase effects in Mozart's music, 167
Ovid, 121

Pope, Alexander, 115
"Purple patches," 5, 103–4

Ratner, Leonard, 122, 176n33, 180n24
Ratz, Erwin, 175n20
Ratzinger, Cardinal Joseph, 181n1
Renewal: in Mozart's music, 117–64; as thematic return in Viennese classical style, 117, 128
Retransition, 128–42; as *Gnade*, 142; with V/vi, 130–33, 139
Romanticism: and consciousness, 114; and interiority 103, 166; and the irrational, 101; and Mozart, 103; role of subject in, 176n38; and visual art, 115
Rosen, Charles, 35–36, 119, 130, 133, 136–37, 173n18, 177n40, 179n1, 180n16, 182n9

Rousseau, Jean-Jacques: and *Essai sur l'origine des langues*, 21
Rückenfigur, 115

Salieri, Antonio, 22
Santayana, George, 100–101
Scarry, Elaine, 171n13
Schaffer, Peter: and *Amadeus*, 22
Schikaneder, Emanuel, 94
Schiller, Friedrich, 7, 142, 166; and "On Naïve and Sentimental Poetry," 101
Schoenberg, Arnold: and *Harmonielehre*, 80; and *Sechs kleine Klavierstücke*, 174n15
Schopenhauer, Arthur, 114
Schubert, Franz, 1, 4, 103, 108, 124; and String Quintet in C, D. 956, 124
Sequences, with root motion by falling fifth: effect of, 133–34, 167, 180n18, 182n9
Shaw, George Bernard, 1
Sisman, Elaine, 125, 179n1, 180n22
Snoopy, 163
Solomon, Maynard, 3, 18–19, 36, 175n21, 176n34, 176n35, 178n50
Sonority: in Mozart's music, 7–19
Subjectivity: post-Kantian, 114; Romantic, 103, 115
Subotnik, Rose Rosengard, 178n52, 181n3

Taruskin, Richard, 179n1, 179n6
Tatum, Art, 3
Tomlinson, Gary, 114
Tovey, Donald Francis, 1, 5, 103, 177n44
Transcendence: and interiority, 114

Wagner, Richard, 1
Weber, Gottfried, 176n28
Webster, James, 176n31
Winter, Robert, 120
Wolff, Christoph, 61, 174n6, 174n9, 174n13
"Word golf," 139